A Manual of Possible Solutions

Third Edition 1981

Edited by:
J. INNES
T.A. LEE
F. MITCHELL

for use with the third edition of
Cases in Auditing Practice

The Institute of Chartered Accountants
in England and Wales

Chartered Accountants' Hall, Moorgate Place, London, EC2P 2BJ

In publishing this book, the Accounting Principles and Auditing Panel of the Technical Services Committee of The Institute of Chartered Accountants in England and Wales considers that it is a worthwhile contribution to discussion, without necessarily sharing the views expressed, which are those of the authors.

No responsibility for loss occasioned to any person acting or refraining from action as a result of any material in this publication can be accepted by the authors or publisher.

The Accounting Principles and Auditing Panel:
Mr J. H. F. Gemmell, CA (Chairman)
Mr R. G. Badger, FCA
Mr B. M. L. Gray, FCA
Mr W. D. R. Swanney, CA

First edition published 1969
Second edition published 1971

© 1981 J. Innes, T. A. Lee and F. Mitchell

ISBN 0 85291 294 3

This book is set Linoterm Times Roman and IBM Press Roman by
R. James Hall Typesetting and Book Production Services
Harpenden Herts and printed by Unwin Brothers Limited
The Gresham Press, Old Woking, Surrey

CONTENTS

Preface

The systems audit

The transactions audit

The year-end audit

General and review cases

PREFACE

This Manual contains possible solutions to the case studies included in the third edition of *Cases in Auditing Practice* published by The Institute of Chartered Accountants in England and Wales.

The editors wish to thank the Institute, the six accounting firms who contributed material for both the Casebook and the Solutions Manual, and the reviewers for their helpful suggestions which have improved this Manual. We are also indebted to Professor Peter Bird for his excellent work in the preparation of the first two editions of the books. For all the solutions the editors take responsibility for any errors and inconsistencies.

Most of the problems in *Cases in Auditing Practice* are such that several different correct or sensible solutions are possible; the published solutions show therefore only one suggested method among several that could have been chosen.

Edinburgh,
July 1981

J. INNES
T. A. LEE
F. MITCHELL

B (2) - NATIONAL PUMPS LIMITED:
FLOWCHART AND REVIEW OF PURCHASES AND
CASH PAYMENT SYSTEMS
ASSIGNMENT 1

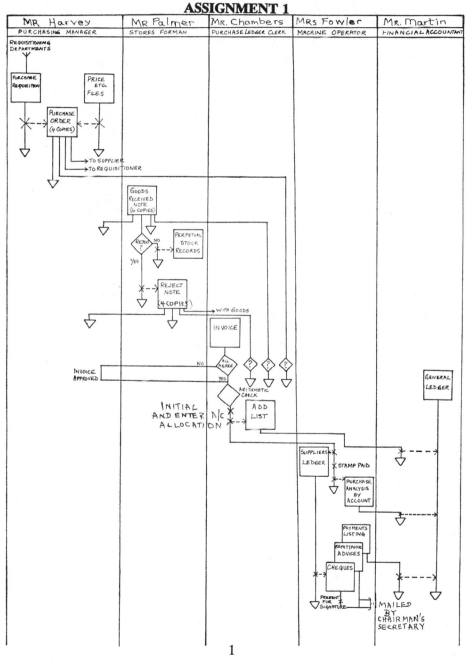

1

ASSIGNMENT 2
SUMMARY OF STRENGTHS AND WEAKNESSES
IN COMPANY CONTROL PROCEDURES

Strengths

(1) Functions of order authorisation and approval, receiving of goods, payment of cash each performed by different employees and are evidenced.

(2) Procedure in force for checking that goods invoiced have been ordered and received, and for dealing with exceptions to this.

(3) Procedure in force for inspection of goods and issue of reject notes where appropriate.

(4) Cheques can only be signed by authorised signatories.

(5) Cheques are mailed immediately after being signed and therefore the possibility of the details on cheques being altered is minimised.

Weaknesses

(1) No supporting documents presented with cheques for signature. As a result lack of adequate check on effective functioning of procedures for ordering, approval, arithmetic checking and account allocation.

(2) Purchasing manager is a cheque signatory (exception to Strength (1) above).

(3) Reject notes are not used as authority to issue and account for debit notes.

(4) Quantities not entered on purchase order when part-deliveries received. May result in lack of control over due completion of delivery.

(5) No reference is made to the sequential numbering of documents such as goods received notes, purchase orders and purchase invoices. It is not therefore possible to account for all items.

(6) Suppliers' statements should be received and reconciled to the suppliers' ledger.

B (3) - MERCURY MERCHANTS LIMITED: ASSESSMENT OF SALES SYSTEM

ASSIGNMENT 1

Strengths

(1) If the invoices are correctly numbered and forwarded by typists (see 1. below)
   (a) All invoices are accounted for, and
   (b) If goods are shipped without an invoice there will be differences on stock records.
(2) All orders *must* become charges to a customer account as order forms and invoices are accounted for.
(3) Physical stock agreed with continuous stock records.
(4) A good division of duties exists.
(5) The sales account is agreed monthly with the sales ledger total.

Weaknesses

(1) Invoices are not pre-numbered. It would be possible for a typist to suppress copies 2, 3, 4 and 5. Goods would then be delivered but no charge would be made to the customer. (It is possible that the warehouse would notice the duplication of numbers, but unlikely).
(2) It appears that there is nothing in the system to provide for a copy invoice to accompany each shipment. This copy should be demanded by the gateman before allowing the consignment to leave the premises.
(3) There appears to be no control of pricing and calculations.
(4) Does anything ensure that five sales invoice copies are identical?
(5) No procedures exist for sales invoices to be finally approved by a responsible official, who at the time of approval should ensure that invoices have been checked in accordance with the company's procedures.

ASSIGNMENT 2

The following errors might be found on checking the raising of sales invoices:

Invoice made out to wrong customer

Quantities and descriptions of goods or service on invoice incorrect

Invoice date incorrect

Incorrect cross referencing between sales invoices and goods outwards or stores records, purchase invoices etc.

No evidence of independent check to ensure that:–

Invoice has been prepared for goods despatched or service given,

quantities and description of goods or service supplied on invoice are correct,

prices and calculations on invoices are correct,

sale approved by credit control,

cost correctly deducted from W.I.P. or stores control.

B (4) - APHIS AND COMPANY LIMITED: INTERNAL CONTROL QUESTIONNAIRE AND APPRAISAL OF CASH SYSTEM

T. McL. & Co.   *Prepared by:*   RBS
                                         Revised by:
Client: Aphis & Company Limited   *Period ended:*   *Date:*   1.1.79

ICQ - Weaknesses
Suggested System

Reference
to ICQ

A.I.(a)(i)   Someone not in the cash department could prepare the credit sales book.

A.I.(d)(ii)   Customer signs red ticket to show he has received the goods.

A.V.(e)(ii)   Foreman retains red tickets in numerical order.
                    Blue tickets are passed on to the Sales Ledger clerk by the foreman.
                    Sales Ledger clerk posts sales ledger from blue tickets.
                    Blue tickets representing cash sales are posted to a cash sales control account in the sales ledger.
                    The present cash sales book posted daily to cash sales control account.
                    The present credit sales book used to post a sales ledger control account in Nominal Ledger.

A.I.(c)(i)
A.V.(e)(iii)   Susie prepares paying-in slip and compares cash banked per paying-in slips to the cash receipts book.

A.I.(a)(ii)
A.I.(d)(i)   Modesty checks for receipt of goods when she numbers the invoices.

A.I.(a)(iii)   Susie helps to make up wages.

A.II.(a)(ii)   Route and time of trips to bank should be varied.

A.II.(d)(i)   Secretary signs remittance advice to show it has been checked.
                    The duplicate copy, without invoices, is passed by the secretary to the cashier.
                    Cashier prepares cheque and enters details in cash book.
                    Cheques returned to secretary who signs those under £1,000.

5

Reference
to I.C.Q.

A.IV.(a)(v) A.IV.(e)	Second cheque signatory stamps invoices 'paid'.
A.I.(c)(iii)	Duties are not segregated.
A.I.(c)(iv)	It has been confirmed that the company's size makes rotation impracticable.
A.II.(d)(ii)	Susie posts cheques.
A.II.(f)	Advantages of a fidelity policy should be pointed out to directors.
A.III.(b)	Keep bank reconciliations for one year.
A.VII.(i)(a)	Secretary should examine reconciliations.
A.IV.(a)(i) and (iii)	Directors sign invoices to show comparison with order and checking of prices.
A.IV.(b)	Cheque books to be locked up.
A.IV.(c)	During holiday periods when all directors are absent give the bank a mandate allowing secretary to draw a maximum amount each week on his own signature alone. This should be sufficient for wages and petty cash. No cheques to be signed in blank.
A.V.(a)(i)	Secretary to keep a cash diary.
A.V.(b)(i) A.VI.(a)	Petty cash should never be reimbursed from cash sales.
A.VI.(b) A.VII.(ii)(a) A.VII.(ii)(b)	Secretary should regularly count petty cash and agree with petty cash book balance.
A.I.(b)	Size of company suggests that having separate petty cashier would not be cost-effective. Common practice to have cash/petty cash kept by same person. System would be satisfactory provided suggestion that secretary makes regular spot checks on petty cash and balance per book is implemented.
A.I.(c)(ii)	Secretary to take money to the bank.
A.II.(a)(i)	If suggestion to vary route and time of trips to bank is implemented, this should go some way towards protection for employees. Case study does not give information on amounts banked daily so possibility of use of, say, Securicor not considered.

Reference
to I.C.Q.

A.II.(c)	Case study does not state whether or not access to office barred to factory workers. If so, then present situation probably acceptable. If not, then suggest partitioning off part of office for cashier use only.
A.VI.(c)(ii)	Secretary to authorise before payment.
A.VI.(e)(iii)	As cashier goes to bank daily, the cheques will be almost immediately converted back into cash, therefore it is felt that it is not necessary in this case to record them.
A.VI.(f)	Not enough information on postages to indicate whether or not a franking machine is necessary.
A.VI.(g)(i) and (ii)	As there are rarely more than two outstanding at any one time, it is considered that recording them on vouchers is adequate.
A.VII.(i)(b)(i) and (ii)	While replies are 'No', suggestion is that Susie prepares paying-in slip. Secretary takes money to bank. Secretary should examine bank reconciliations, would give adequate segregation of duties and check on cashier.
A.VII.(i)(c)(ii) and (iii)	This should be evidenced when secretary examines bank reconciliations.
A.VII(i)(b)(iii)	A request should be made to the bank for reports to be made.

INTERNAL CONTROL QUESTIONNAIRE

(1) The questions have been designed to elicit the answer 'Yes' where control is good. A brief explanation of the facts which justify the answer will often help:

e.g. 'Is the petty cashier a different person from the cashier?'

'Yes. Mr. Jones/Mrs. Robinson.'

Where a question refers to a responsible person, it makes things clearer to give both his name and position.

(2) The questions have been designed to bring out whether the internal control is good or bad, not to build up a complete report of the whole accounting system. Notes and diagrams explaining important and difficult parts of the system should therefore continue to be included in the permanent file.

(3) A separate copy of some sections of the questionnaire may often be conveniently filled in for different branches and departments; likewise for wages and salaries, and raw materials, work in progress and finished goods. The questionnaire is available both in full, bound together, and in individual sections, bound separately.

(4) Answers should preferably be obtained by seeing what actually goes on during the audit. Questions marked with an asterisk should be dealt with by the assistant in charge of the job and generally put to someone senior (e.g. the chief accountant or secretary). It will be understood that tact is required.

(5) The questions suggest the best control that there could theoretically be; in making suggestions for improvement (in part G) assistants should bear in mind what would be reasonable in relation to the size of the business. For example, some segregation of duties is usually practicable, but extensive checking by independent people would presuppose an organisation larger than is customary. Where effective control is achieved by ways not mentioned in the questionnaire – e.g. by the proprietor's close supervision over the day-to-day running of a small business – a note of explanation should be attached to the relevant part.

(6) The internal control of electronic data processing centres is covered in a separate questionnaire.

Part	Prepared by	Date	Revised by	Date	Revised by	Date	Revised by	Date
	(N.B. Use coloured ink for revisions)							
Notes on locations, size and personnel	R.B.S.	1.1.79						
A. Cash	R.B.S.	1.1.79						
B. Wages and salaries	Not applicable to this case study							
C. Purchases and creditors		do						
D. Sales and debtors		do						
E. Stock		do						
F. Fixed assets		do						

8

NOTES ON LOCATIONS, SIZE AND PERSONNEL
(to show the scale of the business and the context
within which the internal control operates)

I. LOCATIONS

Address	Activities	Records prepared at branches (mark with asterisk those not sent to H.O.)	Location covered by H.O. questionnaire (Yes or No)
Maidstone	{ Factory ⎰ Office	⟋ ⟋	⟋ ⟋

II SIZE AND PERSONNEL

	Approx. no. of transactions per period (specify)	Who is in charge?	Who is 2 i/c?	No. of staff in section
Cash	5,000 transactions a year	H. Bristow	–	1
Petty cash	3,000 transactions a year	H. Bristow	–	1
Nominal ledger	£6,000 p.a.	A. Capp	–	1
Wages	60 a week	R. Crock	H. Bristow	2
Salaries	6 monthly excluding directors	A. Capp	–	1
Buying		S. Aphis T. Aphis	— Raw materials — Goods for resale	
Paying creditors	Not applicable to this case study			
Invoicing customers	do			
Collecting debts	do			
Stock recording	do			
Stock custody	do			
Fixed assets records	do			

9

A. CASH

I   SEGREGATION OF DUTIES

Yes or
No

  (a) Do the duties of the cash department
       employees keep them right away from:

       (i)   sales ledgers and records?   *No. Cashier prepares credit sales book*

       (ii) purchase ledgers and records? *No. Cashier checks for receipt of goods*

       (iii) wages and salary records?   *No. Cashier helps to make up wages*

       (iv) nominal ledger and journal?   *Yes*

  (b) Is the petty cashier a different
       person from the cashier?   *No*

       —   do all cash receipts come to the   *N/A*
           cashier, not the petty cashier?

  (c) Do different people do these jobs:

       (i)   prepare the bank pay-in slips?   *No   H. Bristow*

       (ii) take the money to the bank?   *No   H. Bristow*

       (iii) write up the cash book?   *No   H. Bristow*

       (iv) open the incoming mail?   *Yes   A. Capp*

       —   are their duties periodically   *No*
           rotated?

  (d) Are these documents authorised other
       than in the cash department:

       (i)   all those on which cash is paid?   *No {Cashier checks for receipt of goods}*

       (ii) all those as a result of which   *No {Cashier prepares the credit sales book}*
             cash is to be received?

  (e) Are the sales ledger clerks denied access *Yes*
       to cash or cheques received?

II SECURITY (NOTE: all the answers entered below were not specifically covered
                 in the notes)
  *(a) Do trips to the bank ensure:

       (i)   protection for employees en route? *No*

       (ii) variation of route and time?   *No*

10

Yes or
No

(b) Is cash on hand:

   (i) restricted to the minimum? ... ...   *Yes*

   (ii) kept locked in a safe? ... ...   *Yes*

(c) Is the cash department physically segregated from the rest of the office? ... ...   *No*

(d) Are all cheques drawn:

   (i) dispatched immediately they are signed? ... ...   *No. Returned to cashier*

   (ii) without being returned to the cash department? ... ...   *No.*

(e) Are all cheques received immediately crossed 'A/C payee only, not negotiable'? ... ...   *Yes*

*(f) Are all cash department employees covered by a fidelity policy? ... ...   *No*

   Are the company's obligations under the bond observed? ... ...   *N/A*

(g) Is cash on hand and in transit fully insured? ... ...   *Yes*

*(h) Does the company confirm that no employees in the cash department are related to any others? ... ...   *Yes*

*(i) Must at least two week's holiday be taken each year by:

   (i) the cashier? ... ...   *Yes*

   (ii) the petty cashier? ... ...   *Yes*

*(j) Are references in writing obtained direct from previous employers for everyone in the cash department? ... ...   *Yes*

*(k) Have managers and directors made disclosure to the secretary of interests in other businesses with which the company has dealings? ... ...   *Yes*

*(l) Can we confirm that no personal extravagance of any cash department employee has come to our notice during the audit? (Assistants must rely *entirely* on their own observations in answering this question. They must *not* question an official about his own or any other official's personal expenditure.) ... ...   *Yes*

11

Yes or
No

III BANK RECONCILIATIONS

(a) Are they prepared regularly? ... ...   *Yes   Monthly*

(b) Are the detailed workings retained? ... ...   *No   {Kept only to the next reconciliation*

IV CONTROL OF PAYMENTS

(a) Are all payments (by cheque, credit transfer or letter to the bank) supported by vouchers:

                                                   Purchase Ledger   Expenses

    (i) authorised for payment? ... ...   *No   No*

   † (ii) which show that the goods or services have been received?... ...   *Yes   No*

   †(iii) and that the prices and calculations have been checked? ... ...   *No   No*

    (iv) which are submitted to the cheque-signatory? ... ...   *Yes   Yes*

    (v) and which are then cancelled to prevent resubmission? ...   *No – cancelled before submission   No – cancelled before submission*

† These questions may apply only to payments not covered by the purchase invoice system (see C. IV below) – do they? ... ...   *N/A*

(b) Are unused cheque-books kept under lock and key? ... ...   *No*

—   are the cheques accounted for when used, spoiled and cancelled cheques being retained? ... ...   *Yes*

*(c) Is there an absolute prohibition against signing cheques in blank? ... ...   *No   Always happens during and after holidays*

(d) For payments by credit transfers:

    (i) are copies (authenticated by the bank) retained, showing payees and recipient banks? ... ...   *N/A } Not used*

    (ii) does this apply to salary payments also? ... ...   *N/A*

(e) Is it impossible for a voucher to be paid twice? ... ...   *No*

—   why? ... ...   *Already stamped paid when seen by cheque. Signatory.*

		Yes or No
V	**CONTROL OF RECEIPTS**	
	(a) (i) Is there a cash diary?	*No*
	(ii) Does it cover all cheques and cash received in all posts during the day?	*N/A*
	(iii) Is it always prepared by someone other than the cashier?	*N/A*
	(b) Are all cheques and cash received:	
	(i) banked intact?	*No {Occasionally used to reimburse petty cash*
	(ii) on the next practicable working day?	*Yes if banked*
	(c) For retail shops, restaurants, etc. (where cash is taken from the public):	
	(i) do cash registers account for all cash?	*N/A*
	(ii) are the keys to the till rolls held by a responsible person (not a salesman or cashier)?	*N/A*
	(iii) does this responsible person remove the till rolls each day and bank the cash?	*N/A*
	(iv) are the cashiers separate from the salesmen?	*N/A*
	(d) For cash collected by travellers, is it controlled:	
	(i) by a responsible person issuing counterfoil receipt-books?	*N/A*
	(ii) who accounts for their return when completed?	*N/A*
	(iii) and who compares the details with the travellers' collection sheets and bankings?	*N/A*
	(e) For cash and postal orders received directly by the cashier:	
	(i) are pre-numbered counterfoil receipts issued?	*Yes*
	(ii) and are they accounted for by a responsible person?	*No*

13

*Yes or
No*

(iii) who compares the details with
the cash banked? ... ...   *No*

VI PETTY CASH
(a) Is it kept on the imprest system? ... ...   *Yes – float £300*

   – are the only receipts reimbursements
   of the imprest? ... ...   *No – occasionally from cash sales*

(b) Is there evidence that the petty cash
is counted regularly and agreed
with the petty cash book balance? ... ...   *No*

(c) Are all payments:

   (i) supported by vouchers? ... ...   *Yes*

   (ii) which are authorised (before
   payment is made) by someone other than the petty
   cashier? ... ...   *No*

*(d) Are IOUs prohibited ... ...   *Yes*

(e) Are cheques for employees cashed:

   (i) only up to a fixed amount? ... ...   *Yes – £25*

   (ii) are they banked immediately? ... ...   *Yes*

   (iii) are they recorded, showing
   employees' names? ... ...   *No*

(f) Is postage kept separate from petty
cash? ... ...   *Yes – by office girl*

   – is there a franking machine? ... ...   *No*

(g) Are floats for travelling expenses:

   (i) entered in a separate ledger
   account, if permanent? ... ...   *No – not permanent*

   (ii) or in a separate record, showing
   dates of advances and repay-
   ments, if temporary? ... ...   *No – recorded on vouchers*

VII CHECKING BY INDEPENDENT PEOPLE
(i) *On cashier*

*(a) Is there evidence that the bank reconciliations are
periodically checked by someone other than the
cashier? ... ...   *No*

Yes or
No

*(b) Is there evidence that:

    (i)   the bank sends an authenticated duplicate
         pay-in slip to someone other than the   *No*
         person who made out the original? ... ...

    (ii) this is periodically checked by that   *No*
         person against the cashier's records? ... ...

    (iii) the bank reports to this person any   *No*
         credits dishonoured or reversed? ... ...

*(c) Is there evidence that:

    (i)   the bank sends paid cheques and
         statements to someone other   *Yes – the secretary*
         than the cashier? ... ...

    (ii) this person examines paid cheques
         for payees' names and payer's   *No*
         signatures? ... ...

    (iii) and verifies cross-entries,
         cancellations and transfers   *No*
         between bank accounts? ... ...

*(d) Is there evidence that the cash diary is
      periodically checked independently   *N/A – no diary*
      against the cashiers' records? ... ...

(ii) *On petty cashier*

(a) Is there evidence that the petty cash
    books and vouchers are inspected by *No – the vouchers are*
    someone other than the petty cashier *inspected but not*
    before reimbursement? ... ... *the book* ... ...

(b) Is there evidence that the petty cash
    is counted periodically by someone   *No*
    other than the petty cashier? ... ...

    — does this count include *all* the
         funds under the petty cashier's
         control (e.g. employees' funds,
         insurance stamps, unclaimed   *N/A*
         wages, unclaimed tax refunds)? ... ...

(c) Is there evidence that the postage book
    (or record of letters franked) is   *Yes – by the cashier*
    examined by an independent person
    before reimbursement? ... ...

C (1) – SLUSH CONCRETE LIMITED PART II: SALES AUDIT PROGRAMME AND DEBTORS' CONFIRMATION

Manager. . . . .

Senior Assistant . . . .

	Ref to P.F./ Sch. No.	*Extent of check*	*Initials*
V SALES			
(c) *Collection of debts*			
(1) Additions of sales ledger (including carry forwards)		*Ledger Cards* A – D M – Z	*Comp* *Amc*
(2) Test opening balances			... ...
(3) Test sales ledger postings from all sources and scrutinise ledger accounts for identifiability of balance, promptness of cash collections, credit limits, discounts, journal entries, etc. (N.B. One statistical sample)		*Stat. Sample*	*Amc* ... ...
(4) Examine and agree client's reconciliations of detailed balances with control account, seeing regularly performed		*Aug – Oct*	*Amc* ... ...
(5) Examine and test client's age-analysis, ensure that slow-payers are being chased and reported to authority, and that proper provision is being made in interim accounts		*Reviewed with Chief Accountant*	*Amc* ... ...
(6) Confirm sample of balances (or outstanding invoices) direct with customers (first agreeing number and whether positive or negative with manager, and posting statement and/or confirmation request under audit control)		*15 Positive 54 Negative*	*Amc* ... ...

16

Ref to P.F./ Extent of check Initials
Sch. No.

(6)
(cont.)
— agree balances confirmed to
ledger accounts and prove
control balance ... ... *Done* *Amc*

— acknowledge all queries,
get client to clear them,
and verify all reconciling
items and explanations ... ... *Done* *Amc*

— send second requests
(including details of individual invoices where
customer asks for this) ... ... *Done* *Amc*

— verify non-replies by
establishing

(i) goods were ordered

(ii) delivered ... ... *No Non-Replies* *Amc*

(iii) and paid for

— summarise replies
showing percentages ... ... *IV/c/1* *Done* *Amc*

(7) Where there is no sales ledger,
check sample of invoices
examined in V(b) above to
cash received book, and
confirm client's reconcili-
ations of control account ... ... *N/A* *Amc*

(d) *Conclusions*
Summarise weaknesses, errors and
conclusions resulting from above
work ... ... *IV/c/3* *Done* *Amc*

DEBTORS CONFIRMATIONS SUMMARY

		Number	*Value*
Positive			(ex inter company)
(i)	Total trade debtors at 31st October 1983	299	£91,520
	Number of accounts selected for positive confirmation	15	£45,025
	% selected	5%	49.2%
(ii)	Replies		
	Amounts not agreed	Nil	–
	Agreed first time	5	£12,316
	Agreed after reconciliation	10	£32,709
	Failed to reply	Nil	–
		15	£45,025
	Of the above, there replied at second request	4	£6,865

Notes (i) First requests sent 3rd November; second requests 13th November
(ii) Bases of selection 15/30 major accounts > £500 – positive
54/270 of remainder – every 5th A/C – negative

PROBLEMS IN CONFIRMATION REPLIES
(not forming part of above audit schedule – given for information of participants)

(i)   IV/B/16 – failure to delete whichever is inappropriate
IV/B/18 – failure to delete whichever is inappropriate

(ii)   IV/B/19 – reply dated 6.11.83 cash payment of £236.27 made prior to 31.10.83 per customer but not lodged by company until 8.11.83. Why such a long delay?

(iii) IV/B/23 – debtor replies giving indebtedness to GROUP. Confirmation should perhaps be more explicit, though you will always get this sort of reply.

(iv)   IV/B/24 – not signed by debtor. Cash payment of £341.25 made prior to 31.10.83 per customer not lodged until 5.11.83. Why such a long delay?

(v)   IV/B/25 – Sent to SLUSH CONCRETE by mistake. Should we accept this one? OR send second request?

(vi)   IV/B/26 – which firm did he train with, I wonder?

(vii) IV/B/28 – inadequate system to deal with payments in advance

(viii) IV/B/29 – how would we deal with this one?

(ix) The delays in receiving the payments in (ii) and (iv) above should be enquired into. Also the lodgement on 30.10.83 of £332.72 is exactly the net amount claimed by Trollope & Colls to have been paid in October but was not lodged until 5.11.83. This could be a coincidence but it could be evidence of 'teeming and lading'. The original paying-in slips for October and November should be obtained from the bank and compared with the cash book.

POINTS FOR SENIOR AND FOR FINAL AUDIT

Arising on confirmations

(1) Amounts received in advance from customers: there appears to be no system for accounting for this. How does it arise?

(2) Certain of those debtors circularised may subsequently prove bad. Check aging schedule at year-end.

(3) Discounts not allowed – these should be recoverable.

(4) We need to obtain the original paying-in slips from the bank for October and November to compare with the cash book because two of the debtors claimed payments made in October which were not lodged by the company until 5th and 8th November. One of these payments was for £332.72 which is the same amount as a lodgement on 30.10.83. (N.B. In practice, of course, a point like this would have to be cleared immediately, but in the case study this is not possible.)

(5) The credit controller has resigned and has not been replaced. His work is now being done by the sales ledger manager. Credit given has increased from an average of 1.5 months to approximately 2 months at 31.10.83.

(6) The reply from H. Moore Constructors mentions that a claim for defective concrete will be submitted.

Other

(1) Check control account at year-end.
Transposition error in October control.

RECONCILIATION OF CONTROL ACCOUNT WITH SALES LEDGER LISTING – 31ST OCTOBER 1983

Balance as per control		£105,432.79
Less: Error due to transposition in posting from cash book to control		
– as per cash book	£47,617.58	
– as per control	47,167.58	
		(450.00)
Balance as per sales ledger		£104,982.79

19

C (2) – CARMANIA LIMITED: PURCHASES AUDIT PROGRAMME INCLUDING DEPTH TEST

Test (Ref. to Standard audit programme)	Object	Extent of check and basis of selection	Selected from	Sample – verified with/checking carried out
III (a)	To obtain an understanding of the accounting system and the system of internal control and to adapt the standard audit programme where necessary.	N/A	N/A	N/A
III (b) 1	To verify the arithmetical accuracy of the day book	2 months	N/A	N/A
III (b) 2	To verify that entries in the purchase day book are supported by duly authorised invoices or credit notes.	Statistical sample selected at random. Number selected – 50	Entries in purchase day book	Invoices in supplier file in accounts dept. checking that name, date and number are correct, goods are relevant to the company's business and that "control box" thereon has been completed in respect of receipt of goods, order, extensions, coding analysis, authority for payment.
III (b) 3	To verify that all documents within a selected sample exist.	50 of each. Starting no. – selected at random	Orders and GRNs	Numerical sequence verified.
III (b) 4	To confirm our understanding of the system and that it is working satisfactorily	5 invoices for materials 3 invoices for services, consumables etc.	Entries in purchase day book – avoiding very small items.	Orders, requisitions, GRNs, price lists/tenders; verify correct entry made in invoice register and stock ledger.

Ref	Objective	Sample selected	Source	Notes
III (b) 5	as in III (b) 4	3 orders 3 GRN's 3 stock ledger entries 3 purchase returns slips 3 invoice register entries	Orders in buying dept. file of GRN's in cost office. Stock ledger entries. Purchase returns slips in accounts dept. file. Invoice register entries.	Invoices. checking that name and date are correct, goods relevant to company's business, 'control box' has been completed satisfactorily and correct entry made in purchase day book. Ensure all orders properly authorised.
III (b) 6	To verify that the system works where it matters most.	5 invoices for Westcote Steel (principal supplier) Selections of 3 as noted in III (b) 5.	As in III (b) 4 & 5	As in III (b) 4 & 5
III (b) 7	To ensure that all large or unusual items in the purchase day book have been properly authorised and are proper to the company's business	All items in purchase day book > £5,000	Entries in purchase day book	Each large or unusual item should be checked in a manner similar to III (b) 2 above and discussed with senior management as appropriate.
III (b) 8	To record that above tests have been completed satisfactorily	N/A	N/A	As appropriate to each particular point.
III (c) 1	To verify the arithmetical accuracy of the ledger.	25 accounts in full (including carry forward) Selected at random.	Purchase ledger	N/A
III (c) 2	To verify figures brought forward from the previous balance sheet	30 balances selected at random concentrating on large balances	Our record of preceding year's closing balances	Opening balances in this year's purchase ledger.
III (c) 3	To verify the accuracy of the purchase ledger postings	Statistical sample selected at random Number selected – 50	Proportionately from entries in the purchase day book, cash book, journal and other books where appropriate.	The entries in the purchase ledger are correct including dates and references. Confirm journal entries properly authorised.
III (c) 4	To verify that the control account is being used as part of the system of internal control and that any differences are investigated and satisfactorily cleared.	2 months	N/A	Verify reconciling items as appropriate.

21

Test	Object	Extent of check and basis of selection	Selected from	Sample – verified with/checking carried out
III (c) 5	To substantiate that the balances in the ledger are supported by external evidence and that the client is properly controlling the ledger.	30 accounts selected at random concentrating on the large accounts.	Accounts in the purchase ledger	Statements – reconciling items enquired into and verified – confirming that they are reasonable and have been followed up by the client and satisfactorily cleared.
III (d)	To record weaknesses in the system, errors found and their disposal, and to record our conclusions as to the adequacy and accuracy of the records.	N/A	N/A	N/A

OTHER TESTS

Test	Object	Extent of check and basis of selection	Selected from	Sample – verified with/checking carried out
1. Confirm that the purchase day book is reconciled monthly with the invoice register.	To verify that all invoices recorded in the invoice register are properly processed through the system and recorded in the purchase day book; and that satisfactory explanations are received in respect of invoices not yet entered in the purchase day book e.g. not yet approved for payment etc.	2 months	N/A	Verify reconciliations and satisfactorily clear any reconciling items.
2. Check through purchase returns slip file and enquire into and clear satisfactorily the reason for any slips more than two months old on file.	To ensure that company is receiving a credit note in respect of each return.	All slips over 2 months old.	Purchase returns slip file.	Enquire into and receive satisfactory explanation for all slips over 2 months old for which no credit note has been received.

Test	Object	Extent of check and basis of selection	Selected from	Sample – verified with/checking carried out
3. Check a sample of quantity rebates from suppliers for:– a) correct calculation b) receipt of credit notes	To verify that company is receiving proper amounts due in respect of quantity rebates.	1 calendar quarter 3 suppliers giving rebates.	Suppliers giving quantity rebates	Verify credit notes received in respect of quantity rebates as to: a) total purchases for quarter b) 1% calculation c) credit note properly authorised and recorded.

NB : The audit tests on the reconciliation of costing with financial records are covered in the detailed stock audit programme.

PURCHASES – SUGGESTED DEPTH TEST

Invoice no.	Date	Supplier	Goods	Value	Checked To						
					Requisition	Order	Suppliers Price List	Goods Received Note	Stock Ledger	Invoice Register	Purchase Day Book

Basis of selection

5 Raw material purchase invoices at random
3 Services, consumables etc. at random
—
8
—

23

C (3) – CARMANIA LIMITED: AUDIT OF WAGES

(a) Audit Programme

Manager . . . . G. C. C. . . . .
Senior Assistant . . . SRB . . . .

FACTORY WAGES AUDIT PROGRAMME

Y.E. 31.12.1980
Approx. 200 weekly employees

	Extent of check	Department Initials	Extent of check	Department Initials	Extent of check	Department Initials
Preliminary						
(1) Familiarise yourself with the system, the layout of the factory, the Permanent File (bring up to date) and the ICQ, and amend programme as necessary	(N.B. Schedules not given) Done. PAF/ICQ updated	SRB	. . .	. . .	. . .	. . .
(2) Agree with chief accountant the least inconvenient time to do the wages audit (NB Consider value of surprise in wages auditing)	Wednesday.	SRB	. . .	. . .	. . .	. . .
(3) Call for 3 consecutive weeks' clock cards and pay-rolls, and apply tests to middle week (the other two are to explain shift changes, adjustments, etc.) obtained following consecutively. = w.e. 11,18 and 25.7.80	w/e 18/7/80	SRB	. . .	. . .	. . .	. . .
(4) Working from the pay-roll, select names, and pick out and control clock cards for detailed verification (look out especially for names 'tacked on' at the foot of departments)	w/e 18/7/80 Select 20 names at random ('Sch . . .)	SRB	. . .	. . .	. . .	. . .
(5) Obtain copy of current instructions on company's rates and conditions of pay, piece-work and bonus schemes, trade union agreements, overtime rates and authorities, etc.	obtained.	SRB	. . .	. . .	. . .	. . .

I

24

II Verification of Existence

(1) (a) Verify that names on pay-roll are supported by proper clock cards (NB Statistical sample)   *(stat sample (20) from payroll w/e 18/7/80)* w/e 18/7/80 SRB

(b) Give duplicate list of missing cards to wages clerk at *start* of audit   NONE SRB

(c) Inspect all cards for alterations, signatures and authorisation of overtime hours   Inspected — found OK SRB

(2) Reconcile sample of names on pay-roll with details from Personnel and other departments: *(Selected 20 samples at random sch....)*

(a) attendance and absentee records   *(checked with Personnel records).* SRB

(b) records of engagements and dismissals   } *Checked with Personnel dept. files*   SRB

(c) personal files or record cards

(3) Select a sample of names from whole pay-roll (all sections) and confirm with departmental foremen or managers that those employees actually worked for relevant periods (NB Not with foremen collecting pay packets) and NB Use tact!   *(selected 20 names at random sch....)* Done SRB

— satisfactory attendance at the pay-out may be an alternative to this (point VIII (6) below)

III Gross Pay

(a) *Hourly rates*

(1) Agree hours worked on pay-roll with regular and overtime hours printed on clock card   Agreed 20 items selected at random (sch....) SRB

(2) Agree calculation of hours worked at approved rates to give gross pay shown on pay-roll   Agreed as above SRB

	Extent of check	Initials	Department Extent of check	Initials	Department Extent of check	Initials	Department Extent of check	Initials

III Gross Pay

(a) Hourly rates cont.

(3) Vouch rates used with authorities, agreements, etc.

> DONE (as above) SRB

(4) Ensure that all overtime is properly authorised by ~~works manager (or foreman, where allowed to)~~ production control dept.

> Checked authorisation by prod. control dept. on action control dept. on SRB

(b) Piecework and bonus schemes

(1) Agree calculation of work done on ~~job sheet~~ bonus ticket at approved rates to give gross pay shown on pay-roll

> checked to 20 SRB items as above

(2) Vouch rates with authorities, agreements, etc.

> DONE (as above sample) SRB bonus ticket

(3) Ensure that all ~~job sheets~~ bonus ticket are signed by ~~inspector~~ foreman approving work

> DONE - in full for SRB July 80

(4) Check control total of all piecework at agreed rates with total pay-roll (control should be worked out by company before individual pay is calculated)

> N/A - no piecework SRB

(5) Check bonus and incentive payments with details of scheme

> DONE - (20 items SRB as above)

(c) Others

(1) Check all other ingredients of gross pay with authorities, agreements or other evidence (e.g. shift or ~~subsistence~~ allowances, promotion or merit awards, clothing ~~or special allowances~~, etc.)

> Shift and clothing allowances checked SRB for w/e 18/7/80

(d) General

(1) Work out rough average rate of pay (per hour or per job), scrutinise whole pay-roll and enquire into any rates or gross sums which are obviously out of line

> Scrutinised whole payroll - items out of line - discussed and satisfactory answer SRB received (sch...)

IV Deductions

(Selected 20 samples at random per sch...) on sample of **20**

(1) (a) Vouch ~~national insurance~~ deductions with current rates *G.I.* *SRB*
    (see Ministry authorisation for other than full rates) *20 as above*

   (b) Vouch employer's contributions similarly *on sample of 20 as above* *SRB*

(2) Vouch PAYE deductions by checking gross pay to tax
    deduction card, and agreeing with tables and coding notice *Calculation checked* *SRB* *(on above sample of 20)*

(3) Vouch pension fund deductions by checking to pension fund *N/A — no pension*
    record or card, and agreeing amount of contribution with the *scheme in* *SRB*
    rules of the fund *operation*

(4) Vouch savings deductions by checking to employees' account *on sample of 20* *SRB*
    or card in savings department, and seeing employees' authority *as above. OR*

(5) Vouch other deductions similarly with records of entity
    collecting the deductions, and the employees' authority to
    deduct:

   (a)

   (b)

   (c) *NONE*

   (d)

   (e)

(6) Post deductions to ledger accounts and see receipts for
    timeous paying-over of amounts collected *(1) Postings of deductions to ledger—4 weeks in July } SRB* *(2) Payment checked in Aug }*

27

	Department		Department		Department
Extent of check	Initials	Extent of check	Initials	Extent of check	Initials

V Payroll

(1) Check additions, carry forwards, cross casts and summaries *2 months June/July checked with cost dept. record* — SRB
(NB Make sure that total is agreed with cash department records before pay-roll is released)

(2) Net pay vouched with:

  (a) employees' receipts/~~returned cheques/credit transfer list authenticated by bank~~ *100% for w/e 18/7/80* — SRB

  (b) unclaimed wages book *100% June* — SRB

(3) Test some signatures on employees' receipts with personal records *Test checked 4 employees (Jun)* — SRB

(4) Pay-roll approved by officials' signatures *All June examined* — SRB

(5) Total of summaries posted to ledger accounts *June + July* — SRB

VI Advances

(1) Vouch advances with receipts, and confirm in accordance with company's regulations *N/A None allowed* — SRB

(2) Check signatures on receipts with signatures in Personnel Dept. records or later pay-rolls *N/A*

(3) Check that advances paid are deducted from next following pay-roll *N/A*

28

VII Holiday Pay

(1) Select some employees from the pay-roll and list the gross amounts of holiday pay credited to them in the year under review (or paid to them in the previous year, if detailed records not kept) ...... *w/e 8/8/80 6 employees (Sch...) SRB*

(2) Vouch the amount so credited or paid with the rules of the company:

(a) agree calculations ...... *Done (as above) SRB*

(b) verify that employees were engaged throughout the period by reference to Personnel Department records and test with intermediate pay-rolls ...... *Done (") SRB*

(3) Vouch the payments made to these selected employees on the holiday pay-roll, seeing receipts ...... *Done (") SRB*

(4) Agree additions of holiday pay-roll, scrutinise for excessive items and check total to cash records ...... *Done 2 months July/Aug SRB*

(5) Verify provision ...... *Done SRB*

VIII Unclaimed Wages

(1) See that amounts recorded in unclaimed wages book are duly banked on the proper dates (e.g. after one week, etc.) ...... *Checked - never banked, always collected within 1 week or so. SRB*

(2) (a) Select some payments in unclaimed wages book, ~~check~~ ~~to cash records~~ and see receipts *signed by employee* ...... *June SRB*

(b) Agree the signatures on these receipts with those on earlier pay-rolls, or with signed authority to agent to collect on employee's behalf ...... *Done - found OK SRB*

29

		Department		Department		Department	
	Extent of check	Initials	Extent of check	Initials	Extent of check	Initials	Extent of check	Initials

VIII Unclaimed Wages (cont.)

(3) Check additions — *Checked April–June SRB*

(4) See that book is regularly inspected and initialled — *Checked – never inspected by responsible officials SRB*

(5) See that balance of unbanked unclaimed wages is counted at time of cash count *(already in sealed packets – total net wages drawn before the end of each week was vouched with cash book)* — *N/A SRB*

(6) Attend making-up and paying-out, preferably on a surprise basis:

(a) test amounts in pay packets made up and ready for delivery — *5 packets (Sch....) SRB*

(b) check additions on pay-roll and agree net pay with amount drawn from bank — *Done – w/e 8/8/80 June SRB*

(c) accompany wages personnel as they distribute wages packets, and see all packets accounted for — *all packets accounted for SRB*

(d) make close enquiries into any wages packets not claimed — *Done – 2 packets (Sch....) SRB*

IX Conclusions

(1) Summarise weaknesses, errors and conclusions arising from above work — *(see Sch ...) SRB*

C (3) - CARMANIA LIMITED: AUDIT OF WAGES

(b) Outstanding Audit Points

QUERY	RECOMMENDED AUDIT ACTION
(1) The wages clerk advises you that two clock cards, in the names of J. Stein and J. Wallace, cannot be found for the week selected.	(1) (i) Check existence/attendance with personnel department records
	(ii) Examine previous and subsequent week's clock cards for these employees and enquire into any material variation in hours worked.
	(iii) Compare hours worked by these employees with similar grade of employee in same gang/shop.
	(iv) Enquire into reasons for this breakdown in system and amend audit programme accordingly. Satisfy yourself that no further detailed work needs to be done.
(2) D. Revie is paid for one hour of travelling time per day but this is not shown on his personal record card.	(2) This should be confirmed by a responsible official and personnel department instructed to amend record card accordingly.
(3) According to his clock card G. Best worked for 70 hours in one week.	(3) (i) Confirm clock card countersigned by foreman.
	(ii) Find out from the production control department the reason for such large amount of overtime — rush job, shortage of staff through illness etc.?
(4) PAYE card for D. Law shows 'Tax due to date' £1.20 too much and therefore employee suffered this additional deduction.	(4) (i) Check following week to ensure that PAYE is now adjusted to normal.

31

QUERY	RECOMMENDED AUDIT ACTION
	(ii) To ensure that it is only an isolated clerical error and not an error of principle — check 5 more cards (selected at random) for different weeks.
(5) R. Charlton has been paid 4 hours too much (£4.50) under the bonus system due to error in calculating bonus hours.	(5) (i) Discuss with wages clerk. If he agrees the error but is unwilling to correct it in the following week, then discuss with works manager. If the works manager suggests that to recover this amount would cause industrial unrest etc. forget it.
	(ii) But check a few more calculations in the same week to ensure that the above is an isolated non-recurring error of calculation.
	The management letter should suggest that the calculations of the wages clerk *must* be cross checked by another member of staff in the wages department to ensure correct deductions etc.
(6) Employees in Shop 3 are paid an average rate of £1.20 per hour but R. Moore is being paid £1.40 per hour.	(6) Discuss with wages clerk and works manager; if found to be for special responsibilities/skill etc., then inspect some sort of written authorisation.
(7) During your examination of the clock cards for the selected week, the writing appeared to be the same for B. Bremner and J. Giles.	(7) Examine previous week's signatures. Check the signatures on the clock cards to the specimen signatures on the employees' personnel files (e.g. on the contract of employment). If different, discuss with works manager and if necessary, raise in the management letter.
(8) Some names were written in pencil in the payroll. The wages clerk explained that they started work in the middle of last week but the wages sheets were typed at the beginning of the previous week (wages being paid one week in arrears).	(8) (i) Ink the names before inserting audit ticks.
	(ii) Check with the personnel department's records to check the exact date of commencement of their duties, rates etc.

QUERY	RECOMMENDED AUDIT ACTION
	(iii) Check the entries on the clock card and reconcile the figures in the wages sheet.
(9) Some of the names as mentioned in point No. 8 above could not be traced in the following week's wages sheet — wages clerk explained that those individuals had not turned up for their duties any more.	(9) (i) Check with personnel department's records to ensure that the fact was notified to them and the same was (recorded) in the individual's file.
	(ii) Check whether P.45 was prepared by the wages department and kept in the file (the same may have to be sent to the new employer if asked for).
	(iii) Scrutinise a few weeks wages sheets and see whether same names appear again.
(10) While scrutinising the whole payroll, the following names were spotted in week ending 30.7.80. Mr S Jones Mr L Carter Mr M Smith Gross wages amounting to £900 were paid without any deductions at all — wages clerk explained that the above individuals are labour sub-contractors working on their own mainly to dispose of industrial refuse, scrap etc. from various factories in the area.	(10) (i) Check that the use of the labour sub-contractors was authorised by the works manager.
	(ii) Check the receipts/exemption certificates which should have been produced by the above individuals when receiving gross payments.
	(iii) If the certificates were not produced, Income Tax at the standard rate should have been deducted from the gross payment and been paid over to the Revenue.
	(iv) If the certificates were not produced report it to the works manager and explain the correct procedure. Include the item in the management letter. Check to ensure that these were isolated payments and not recurring.

QUERY	RECOMMENDED AUDIT ACTION

(11) Wages unclaimed — 6 weeks — 2 packets.
 	
    It was suggested that the packets be opened for our inspection — to ensure that they actually contained the amount as stated on the front of the packets. The works manager took great exception to this and refused to open the packets.
	(11) (i) Find out the reason for not banking these unclaimed wages for such a long period of time.
	
	    (ii) Explain to works manager that the checking of the contents of the unclaimed wages packets (which were not collected within a reasonable period of time) is a part of your routine audit test.
	    It is not a reflection of any individual's integrity (use tact.)
	    This should usually work. Then check the contents of the packets in the presence of the works manager.
	    Point for management letter.

C (3) - CARMANIA LIMITED: AUDIT OF WAGES

(c) Payroll Vouching

A Gross pay in a service company

(1) *Clock hours*

Employees may be required to clock on and off at their base depot or other branches, but it is much more likely that a time sheet authorised by a supervisor will be the only evidence of hours worked.

(2) *Hourly rate*

This should be recorded on each employee's personnel record. It should agree to the company's agreed rate for the grade or status of job concerned.

(3) *Basic and travelling pay*

The total hours worked are split between basic hours and travelling, according to the time sheet. This document should be checked to see that the analysis has been correctly made. The basic hours will be paid at the hourly rate, and travelling hours may be paid at this or a lower rate as defined by the contract of employment, which should be examined.

(4) *Overtime premium*

The overtime premium represents the additional hours allowed for payment as compensation for work outside normal hours. Allowances of 33%, 50% and 100% are usual, with the highest rate being allowed for work on Saturdays or Sundays.

The company's rules should be ascertained and the time at which extra hours were worked should be checked to the time sheet and seen to be authorised.

(5) (a) *Holiday pay*

The critical factors on which holiday pay is based are the company's entitlement rules and the individual's eligibility based on service and holiday credits earned.

It is necessary to ascertain how much holiday the employee is entitled to with pay, whether the holiday taken is within this limit, and whether the employee has been paid at the correct rate.

(b) *Holiday credit*

The holiday credit system is operated to maintain a record of an employee's holiday pay entitlement as it accumulates week by week. This is necessary when employees have their entitlement reduced due to absenteeism.

(5) (c) *Holiday reserve*

This shows the accumulated effect of each employee's holiday credits, less the amount of holiday pay drawn. Companies usually operate a holiday pay year which ends just before the summer holiday period. A typical situation would be for a company to have a holiday year end of 30 June, and holiday rules permitting four weeks holiday in total, with two weeks to be taken during the holiday year, and two weeks after the 30 June, e.g. a week at Christmas, a week in autumn or spring, and two weeks after 30 June.

(6) *Bonus and other pay*

Bonuses and other pay increments can only be verified from a detailed knowledge of the circumstances. Find out what the bonus is for, check that it has been properly authorised and confirm that the amount paid is based on the correct facts.

B Gross pay in a manufacturing company

(1) *Clock hours*

In almost all cases these will be evidenced by clock cards. When overtime has been worked it should be authorised by the departmental manager initialling clock cards, or otherwise advising the wages office in writing.

(2) *Hourly rate*

See A(2)

(3) *Basic pay*

This is calculated from the actual hours worked at the basic hourly rate.

(4) *Overtime premium*

See A(4)

(5) *Piecework earnings*

These can either be evaluated directly, or as in the system illustrated, work performed can be assessed in standard hours which are paid at the normal hourly rate. In either case it is necessary for the auditor checking the pay to examine the labour or job cards to confirm the work actually done and to check that the work done on each job has been evaluated at the established rate for the job.

(6) *Down-time*

When there is no work available for a pieceworker to perform, or some time must be spent maintaining a machine the employee is paid at an hourly rate. Time thus spent is evidenced by clock cards or time sheets. It is important that the charging of hours to down-time is carefully controlled and authorised, since if an employee commenced work on a job before being booked off the down-time card, he would in effect be paid twice.

(7) *Shift premium*

When shift working is employed it is usual to keep rates of pay for jobs the same, and to compensate those employees who work unsocial hours by the payment of a premium for each shift worked. The auditor should obtain a list of the premiums allowed for each shift, and confirm by examination of the clock cards that employees receive the allowance worked for the appropriate shift.

(8) *Bonus and other pay*

See A(6)

(9) *Holiday pay*

See A(5)

C. Payroll deductions

(1) *PAYE*

Income tax is deducted at source from all employees. The tax withheld each period is determined by the tax code number, which is advised to the company by the local tax office on a form which should be retained. The tax calculation is easily checked using tax tables but since the deduction is calculated on a cumulative basis the gross pay and tax to date have to be obtained from the previous payroll to complete the check.

(2) *National Insurance*

This is levied as a percentage of the gross pay between upper and lower limits. A Government leaflet should be consulted to ascertain the rate and limits currently in force.

(3) *Court Order*

An instruction to deduct a sum of money for a specified period is received from the clerk to the court. This instruction, together with the receipts received from the court, are the documents to which the deduction may be vouched.

(4) *Voluntary deductions*

It should be noted that all deductions other than those shown above can only be made if the employee has given his consent in writing. Some companies are now using comprehensive contracts of employment on which miscellaneous deductions are listed and authorised by the employee's signature. The authority for each deduction should be checked by the auditor.

(a) *Company pension*

The amount deducted should be checked to the rules of the scheme and the employee seen to be an eligible member.

(4) (b) *Loan repayment*

The loan receipt should be inspected and the amount deducted seen to be in agreement with the repayment terms.

(c) *Union dues, Savings, Hospital fund* (private health insurance)

The amount of each deduction should be checked to the employee's authority. The payment by the company to the outside body should be confirmed by examining a copy of the list sent with the remittance, detailing individual contributors.

(d) *Social club, Charitable donations, Overall cleaning*

The amount of the deduction should be checked to the leaflets detailing the relevant scheme.

(5) *Net pay adjustment*

This is a method used in many payrolls at present to adjust the net pay to a multiple of 50 pence. This saves time in the making up of pay packets and 'coin analysis' since only notes and 50p pieces are used. Wages are usually rounded up to the 50p above, the amount advanced for the rounding being deducted from the following weeks net pay before the rounding up is repeated.

In the example shown on the pay slip the actual net pay is £79.80, if there was no adjustment from the previous week the employee would be advanced 20p. If in the following week the actual net pay is £84.16, 20p is deducted and the current week adjustment is 4p with £84.00 being paid out.

C (4) - PRACTICAL SAMPLING LIMITED: STATISTICAL SAMPLING

A Determining the monetary precision

(1)   Monetary precision (MP) should be set according to our judgement of the maximum monetary amount of error that we consider to be not material in relation to the accounts as a whole. Since judgement differs from one person to another, there can be no 'correct' answer, and the partner in charge of an audit will accept responsibility for determining the MP. It is the task of the accountant in charge (AIC) to obtain the necessary information to enable the partner to reach a rational decision.

(2)   Practical Sampling Ltd.'s business is expanding rapidly, with sales in the six months to 30 June 1988 exceeding those for the whole of 1987. Clearly, therefore, it would not be satisfactory to base the MP solely on the 1987 figures. The AIC of the audit should try to obtain an estimate of the likely results for 1988. To this end, he should review the company's budgets, testing their accuracy by reference to the recorded results for the first half of 1988. If formal budgets are not prepared the AIC should obtain what information he can by interviewing the client's management.

(3)   Let us suppose that the AIC's review of the management's projections to 31 December 1988 justifies the following assumptions :

(a) that the upsurge in business will neither gain nor lose momentum in the second half of 1988, and

(b) that seasonal factors are not important.

Based on these assumptions, the results for 1988 might be as follows :

	1988 (Estimated) £000	1987 (Actual) £000	1986 (Actual) £000
Sales	2,725	1,014	861
Profit before tax	220	130	101
Net assets	1,000	976	960

(4)   In the absence of any special circumstances affecting materiality, the MP for a manufacturing or trading concern should normally be set within the limits :

    5% to 10% of profit before tax
    and
    ½% to 1% of sales.
In this case the limits would be :

    5% to 10% of profit before tax = £11,000 to £22,000
    ½% to 1% of sales   = £13, 625 to £27,250

On these figures, an MP in the range £15,000 to £20,000 would seem to be reasonable. An error of £20,000 would probably just be tolerable in relation to pre-tax profit and would not seriously distort the steep upward trend of profits. However, if we consider the management's forecasts for 1988 to be unduly optimistic we would scale down the MP accordingly.

(5)   The final choice of MP should take account of all the relevant circumstances, including the following :

(a) factors which cause the view given by the accounts to be more than usually sensitive to comparatively small mis-statements, such as :

the trend of profits
the net current asset position
the liquidity ratio

(b) circumstances which are likely to lead to the accounts being relied on in an especially critical decision, such as a take-over situation.

(c) the likelihood of errors being found which, on evaluation, would tend to increase the MP to an unacceptably high level.

B Accounts to be included in the transactions sample

(6)   In the annotated version of the trial balance set out opposite, the symbols indicate the following :

T : that the account is to be included in the sample of transactions.
B : that the account is instead to be tested by the 'balance' method.

Notes I to VIII that follow the trial balance explain the reasons for the methods selected for certain of the accounts.

Trial balance – 30/6/88

	Notes		Dr	Cr
Advertising		T	30,826	
Audit		T	4,000	
Bad debts		T	12,217	
Carriage		T	32,465	
Cost of sales	I	Separate	953,735	
Creditors		B		1,017,206
Debentures		B		400,000
Debenture interest	II	T (Special)	20,000	
Debtors		B	1,114,273	
Depreciation		T	48,000	
Deferred taxation		B		67,000
Discount received	IV	T		33,324
Fixtures and fittings	VII	T	84,317	
– depreciation		T		36,749
General expenses		T	7,925	
Insurance		T	12,300	
Interest paid	III	T	5,751	
Leasehold Property	VII	T	275,000	
– amortisation		T		42,500
Legal and professional fees		T	4,020	
PAYE	V	T		13,617
Pension scheme	V	T		3,902
Plant and machinery	VII	T	817,609	
– depreciation		T		264,203
Power		T	6,124	
Rent and rates	III	T	23,127	
Retained earnings		B		219,714
Salaries and wages	VI	Separate	125,486	
Sales	IV	T		1,362,478
Share capital		B		500,000
Share premium		B		256,000
Stock	I	T	1,273,954	
Suspense	VIII	T	720	
Taxation		B		86,529
VAT	V	T		46,178
Cash book		B		502,449
			£4,851,849	£4,851,849

NOTES

I Cost of sales, and stock

Paragraph 3(b) of the case study states that 30% of the proceeds of sale represent gross profit. Therefore, the cost of sales figure (£953,735) should be 70% of the sales (£1,362,478), which it is. All the debits to the cost of sales account are thus transfers from stock account. Consequently, there is no need to sample the cost of sales account since we can satisfy ourselves quickly about all the entries in the account by :

(a) Agreeing the debits in the account with the corresponding credits in the stock account, and

(b) Checking the casts of the account and checking that the total cost of sales is 70% of the total sales.

We therefore exclude the cost of sales account from the general ledger debit sample. (Note : If the transfers from stock account cannot be easily identified, or if the cost of sales account contains debit entries from other sources, the cost of sales account should be included in the debit sample. Each debit entry selected should be checked to the corresponding credit in the stock account or, if it is not a stock transfer, should be otherwise verified as appropriate. It is not necessary to trace a debit back to a purchase invoice, unless purchases can by-pass the usual procedure of being debited initially to the stock account.)

Stock account is included in the general ledger debit sample. We will check each debit entry selected, by examining the purchase invoice, the goods received record, the purchase order, etc.

II Debenture interest

Debenture interest is the classic example of the 'proof in total technique'. Proof in total means proving the total figure on an account exactly by reference to independent factors. Thus, in this example we can prove correctness of the £20,000 debenture interest for the half-year because it represents the half-yearly payment on the £400,000 debentures at 10% per annum. If we allow an R-factor of 3.0 for an exact proof in total, this leaves only the minimum R-factor of 0.5 to be obtained from our sample. For this reason it is probably more economical for us to sample the account separately, since the remaining accounts will have an R-factor of at least 1.0 for detailed testing.

III Interest paid, and rent and rates

The considerations outlined in II above might apply in some instances to interest and rents and also to dividends payable. In this case, the interest cannot be proved in total because it was interest on a fluctuating bank over-draft. It might well be possible to prove the rents in total, but the combined rent and rates account makes it awkward to include only the rates element in the general ledger debit sample. Consequently, both interest and rent and rates are included in the debit sample.

IV Discounts received, and sales

Although most of the transactions in these accounts are credit entries (which we will audit for understatement) we must not forget to include any debit entries in our general ledger debit sample. The firm's sample selection schedules are designed to ensure that such items are not overlooked.

V PAYE, Pension scheme, and VAT

It is difficult to test these 'holding' accounts by the 'balance' method since the balances will normally be credits and must therefore be tested for under-statement.

Therefore, it is usually more convenient to include these accounts in the transactions sample. The debit entries selected in the sample will mainly be payments, and we will ensure that these have been made to the correct authority (by examining cheques, receipts, etc.). (Note : The credit entries will be tested for understatement by selecting from the appropriate source of the transactions, i.e. the payrolls and the sales records.)

VI Salaries and wages

Theoretically, salaries and wages can be included in the general ledger debit sample. However, this often results in one or more items being selected from each payroll period and is thus a cumbersome and time consuming approach to auditing payrolls. Usually, the most effective and economical way to audit a payroll where the internal control is good is the payroll selection reconciliation technique. This entails :

(a) detailed tests of three payroll periods, and
(b) detailed analytical review of the remaining payroll periods, including a comparison of those periods with the period(s) tested in detail.

This technique is assumed to be appropriate for this case study. Thus, the salaries and wages accounts are excluded from the general ledger debit sample. (Note : This approach is appropriate where (as is usual) salary and wage costs are stable, varying little from one period to the next. It is not necessarily appropriate where the client's level of activity, and thus its payroll, varies considerably.)

VII Plant and machinery, fixtures and fittings, and leasehold property

Since it is necessary to examine additions to fixed asset accounts at some stage during the audit it is usual to include these accounts in the transactions sample. We select from the opening balance plus the additions during the year, and we can use this sample for several purposes :

(a) to verify existence and ownership of the items selected, or alternatively to verify the proceeds if they have been disposed of
(b) to check the additions with the supporting invoices, capital sanctions, etc.
(c) to check that the items selected have been correctly depreciated—a test for under-statement of the provision for depreciation.

VIII Suspense

The suspense account is included in the transactions sample on the assumption that the transactions passing through it are not significant. However, it is probably advisable to confirm this beforehand by looking at the ledger account. This will enable us to determine whether the account should be audited as part of the transactions sample or in some other way.

C (5)(a) - E.D. PAYMENTS LIMITED: COMPUTER AUDITING

Manual system

In this system the persons preparing cheques were Mike Shell, who matched backing documents and prepared the cheque payments list, and Graham White who physically prepared the cheques.

Computer system

Mike Shell no longer matches backing documents and Graham White no longer prepares cheques. In fact EDP has complete control over the payments process and so the EDP function should be analysed to see if any one person in EDP could circumvent the matching procedure and produce an unauthorised cheque.

C (5)(b) – SYSCO LIMITED: COMPUTER AUDITING

Commentary on flowchart overleaf

Completeness of data

Not all data may be posted to the general ledger because:
(i) there is no check to ensure that all batches created appear on the accepted or rejected batches reports. Therefore a batch may be lost in transit between the accounts supervisor and the data controller. It would be better if the computer kept a check on batch numbers and reported any gaps in the sequence.
(ii) there is no check to ensure that all previously rejected batches are re-submitted. The rejection reports should also list all rejected batches from previous weeks.

Accuracy of data

Not all data may be accurately posted because there is no formal check on the accounts codes used by accounts clerks. Only items with codes which do not exist will be rejected by the system. The supervisor should formally scrutinize all codes. If budgetary control procedures were in operation the computer could report on actual balances compared to budgeted values.

Authorisation of data

All data is authorised because the supervisor signs posting notes and the signature is checked by the data controller.

GENERAL LEDGER SYSTEM FLOWCHART (see commentary on p.45)

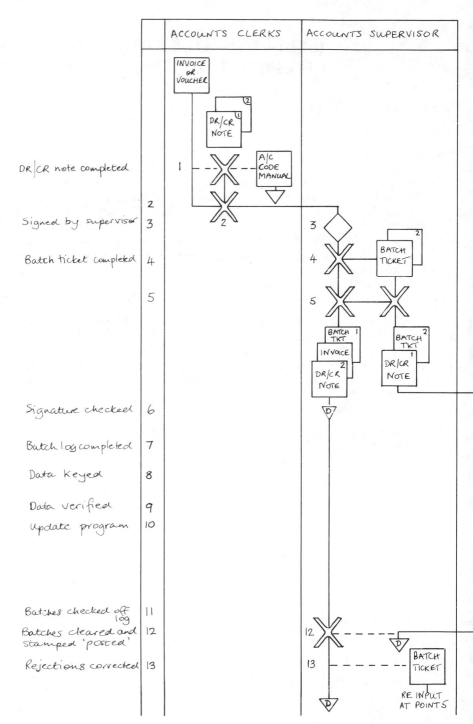

DATA CONTROLLER	DATA PREPARATION	EDP PROCESSING

C (5)(c) - BLIND FAITH BANKING LIMITED: COMPUTER AUDITING

In this case the bureau has access to both records and assets—money owed to the bank on overdrawn balances and loans. An employee of the bureau might open an account with the bank in the normal course of business. It is very unlikely that the bank could prevent or detect this happening since a false name or a relative's name might be used. The employee then has potential to:

(a) teem and lade on his account
(b) overdraw his account beyond an acceptable limit
(c) suppress interest charges.

The circumstances which could lead to this are:

(a) Data preparation staff could deliberately spoil or amend batches so that their own cheques are continually cycling through the suspense accounts, or through other customers' accounts.
(b) Operators may be able to introduce interest rate change or overdraft limit change notices to update their own accounts and then destroy the relevant update reports. In most banking systems details of customers' overdraft balances are not printed out unless the authorised limit is approached. A limit of say £9,000,000 would be useful to anyone.
(c) Programmers or operators may be able to amend programs so that although unauthorised events take place on their accounts, they are not reported by the programs.

D (1) - SLUSH CONCRETE LIMITED PART III: YEAR-END AUDIT OF DEBTORS

Debtors lead schedule	*1983*	*1982*
*Turnover**	£594,317	£472,965
Trade debtors	96,853	61,462
Prepayments	1,025	730
Sundry debtors	12,105	9,260
	£109,983	£71,452

*excluding intercompany sales

Ratios	Debtors: Sales % (months)	16.2% (2 months)	12.8% (1½ months)
	Bad debts: Sales %	0.80%	0.54%

Trade Debtors

Balance as per sales ledger			£114,377.04
Add:	Credit balances on sales ledger	£164.26	
	Debit balances on purchases ledger	245.69	
			409.95
			114,786.99
Less:	Provisions and write offs		
	Bad debts	3,888.14	
	Doubtful debts	875.34	
	Claims	1,742.92	
			(6,506.40)
			108,280.59
Less:	Provision for discount allowed		(1,400.00)
			106,880.59
Less:	MoConCoy – Intercompany balance		(10,027.36)
			£96,853.23

49

Schedule of adjustments made to clients' accounts

Trade debtors per clients' schedule	£106,387.27
Transfer inter-company balance	(10,027.36)
Discount not posted	(946.32)
Reduction in bad debts provision	554.55
Cr. balances and Dr. balances on purchases ledger	
transferred to/from creditors	409.95
Payment in advance transferred to creditors	475.14
Total as above	£96,853.23

Note: *Contra accounts not eliminated (315.52) as they were not considered to be material.*

Provision for Doubtful Debts

Basis:	25% on balances October and before		
	October		£3,904.64
	September and before		4,169.42
			8,074.06
Add:	Credit balances	£ 84.32	
		1.76	
			86.08
			8,160.14
Less:	Intercompany balances	429.17	
		1,925.32	
			(2,354.49)
			5,815.65*
Less:	Amounts written off		
	Cement Marketing	16.06	
	North Bradley	601.72	
	Twycon	19.94	
	Balances under £100	472.37	
	(September and before)		(1,110.09)
			4,705.56
Less:	Cement Marketing Board		
	October balance considered safe		(1,204.19)
			£3,501.37
	Whereon 25% provision		£ 875.34

50

Review Notes:

(1) *Addition error is immaterial.

(2) Basis of provision for doubtful debts is considered reasonable. November and December balances have been considered for recoverability during the review of doubtful debts.

Reconciliation of Control A/C & Sales Ledger

Balance as per CONTROL A/C		£109,560.08
Less: Discount not posted		946.32
		108,613.76
Add: Bad debts written off, included in sales ledger		3,888.14
		112,501.90
Add: Amount paid in advance – to be included in sundry creditors	£ 475.14	
Provision for discount allowed	1,400.00	
		1,875.14
Balance as per SALES LEDGER		£114,377.04

Interest Payable Suspense Account

Check on prepayment and charge to profit and loss account

	A	B	C	D	E		
Year of agreement	Capital	Interest	Total payable under agreement	Instalments paid in 1983	Instalments o/s at 31.10.83	Interest suspense at 31.10.83 $(B \times E / C)$	Charge to P & L account $(B \times D / C)$
	£	£	£	£	£	£	£
1983	20,000	9,000	29,000	4,200	24,800	7,697	1,303
1982	18,000	6,480	24,480	8,160	12,200	3,229	2,160
1981	15,000	4,950	19,950	6,650	4,000	992	1,650
1980	22,000	6,600	28,600	4,800	–	–	1,108
				£41,000		£11,918	£6,221
Per accounts						£12,000	£6,200

Difference due to rounding—not material

Manager. . . . .

Senior assistant . *S.G* . . . . . .

	Sch. No.	Extent of check	Initials

X DEBTORS   *References not given here)*

  (a) *System*

    Read PF and ICQ, review system and
adapt programme as necessary   ... ...   *Done*   *AMC*

  (b) *Trade*

    (1) For at least last month of year,
examine and agree client's reconciliations of detailed balances
with control account, post control account and vouch any
journal entry   ... ...   *Nov 1983*   *AMC*

    (2) Test extraction of closing balances,
scrutinising for promptness of payment, composition of balance, etc.
and noting doubtful items (NB Where
there is no sales ledger, test analysis
of closing balance with invoices
rendered before, and with those paid
after, date)   ... ...   *All a/cs 7 £500 and for remainder every 5th a/c*   *AMC*

    (3) Verify large credit balances, and
explain   ... ...   *No large ones*   *AMC*

    (4) Select some material sales towards
end of period and verify that goods
were delivered or service rendered
before the year-end   ... ...   *5 sales in w/e 31/12/83*   *AMC*

    (5) Obtain client's aging schedule,
test and summarise, comparing
with previous year and bringing
out sales/debtors ratio   ... ...   *Checked 15 a/cs over £2000*   *AMC*

    (6) Verify client's provision for bad
and doubtful debts, ensuring that
items noted in step 2 above are
included, verifying ECGD and
insurance arrangements, and
obtain explanations from respon-
sible official   ... ...   *In full*   *AMC*

    (7) Verify and explain basis of pro-
visions for discounts, rebates,
allowances and claims, return-
able packages, etc.   ... ...   *See Schedule*

Sch. No. Extent of check Initials

    – examine credit notes and goods
      returned records in new year, and
      see provided for where material . . .   . . .   *Examined to 25/1/83*   *AMC*

(8) Test and note outstanding balances
     on schedule with receipts after date,
     tracing a few items into the bank
     pass sheets via customers' remittance
     advices   . . .   . . .   *30 a/cs of Which 10 > £500 20 < £500*   *AMC*

(9) (a) if confirmation satisfactorily
        completed at interim

        – examine control account since
          then, and vouch large or unusual
          items   . . .   . . .   *Nov & Dec*   *AMC*

        – select a few large year-end
          balances, send positive con-
          firmations, and pursue relent-
          lessly   . . .   . . .   *5 balances over £4000*   *AMC*

     (b) If confirmation *not* satis-
        factorily completed at
        interim, do now   . . .   .   *N/A*

(10) Eliminate contra balances only
      if material   . . .   . . .   *Not material on client's*   *AMC*

(11) Schedule balances in excess of 5%
      of total   . . .   . . .   *Schedule*   *AMC*

(c) *Loans and employees' accounts*
    (on test basis if numerous)

    (1) Agree extraction of balances,
        scrutinising for prompt payment
        ~~and agree with control~~   . . .   . . .   *In full.*   *AMC*

    (2) Verify that repayments are being
        made in accordance with terms
        of loans, and test interest
        calculations *(interest - free)*   . . .   . . .   *In full*   *AMC*

        – test receipts after date to
          remittance advice and bank
          statements   . . .   . . .   *In full*   *AMC*

    (3) Vouch additional amounts ad-
        vanced during the year with
        receipts, authorities, etc.   . . .   . . .   *In full*   *AMC*

Sch. No. *Extent of check* *Initials*

(4) Verify existence of security
held, and compare value with
outstanding balance ... ... *No security* AMC

(5) Obtain certificates of balances
direct from the debtors ... ... *In full* AMC

(6) Agree provision ... ... *None* AMC

(d) *Prepayments*
(1) Schedule and explain amounts
prepaid, indicating (a) how
arrived at and (b) how verified
(if material) *(prepared by client)* ... ... *In full* AMC

(2) Scrutinise last month of cash
book and purchase journal to
ensure that all major prepay-
ments have been picked up ... ... *Dec 1983 In full* AMC

(3) Obtain confirmation of material
deposits ... ... *None* AMC

(4) Compare with previous years,
tie in with P & L and account
for major fluctuations ... ... *See Schedule* AMC

(e) ~~Bills~~ *Orders in progress* ① *Obtain year-end listing and add it.* *In full* AMC
~~Where significant, write and complete~~
suitable programme covering verifica- ② *Vouch listing with subsequent* *10 out of 35 incomplete orders* AMC
tion of existence at year-end, prompt-
ness of payment, interest, credit- *receipts of weekly returns and*
worthiness, dishonoured or renewed *weigh tickets*
bills, ~~ECGD~~ cover and amount dis- ③ *Consider claims* *None required* AMC
~~counted (contingent liability)~~ *for defective concrete*

(f) *Conclusions*
Summarise weaknesses, errors and *Notes for manager* *As noted* AMC
conclusions resulting from above work ... ...

Notes for Senior
(and to consider for management letter)

(i) There was a large increase in the total of credit notes issued in
November (£5,200 against normal month of £200). The sales ledger manager's
explanation is that a mistake was made in posting invoices in that month which
necessitated these being credited and reposted. However, I do not accept this
because the net sales for that month amount to £51,000 but the age analysis of

the balances at 31.12.83 shows November sales outstanding of £52,600. Furthermore, in the age analysis at 31.10.83 an amount of £1,241.14 in the Cement Marketing Board account is classified as August sales but there is a similar amount shown as November sales in the December aging list. I think the sales ledger manager (who is now responsible for credit control) has updated the aging schedules by issuing credit notes against old invoices and recharging these as November sales. (N.B. In practice you would of course follow up this point by examining the credit notes and ledger cards but the necessary information to enable you to do this has not been given in the case study.)

(ii)   Client's working papers mostly incorrect. Basic errors of principle involved.

(iii)   As at the interim, control account had to be reconciled with sales ledger. As client prepared his working papers on the basis of the control account balance, it seems obvious that no-one is checking the control account to the ledger balance, i.e. the control is worthless.

(iv)   Company not prepared to chase discount wrongly taken.

(v)   Still manged to trade with North Bradley Constructors after bankruptcy notice in Gazette (first having verified that there were not incomplete orders at 30.11.83, billed in December). This confirms what we said about the credit control following the interim audit.

(vi)   Ventro Ferazzo, etc.—no-one really authorised the 'special discount' of 5% compared with 2½% as per permanent file.

(vii)   A/C98—Crete Con Agents. Failure of credit control department—balance gone bad is in excess of credit limit—further confirmation of lack of effective credit control system.

(viii)   There is the usual defective concrete claim from Henry Moore (see also confirmation reply at interim). Is he perhaps being sent the wrong mixture? (The specification shown on his original order being destroyed by the sales office after making up the standard order.)

(ix)   Inadequate system to record payments in advance.

(x)   Debtors turnover ratio up—1½ months in 1982
                              —2 months in 1983
no apparent reason—credit control again etc.

D (2) - REBEL (G.B.) LIMITED:
AUDIT OF FIXED ASSETS

Adjusting Journal Entries

			£	£
Dr. Repairs and renewals	A/C 550		1,163	
Plant and machinery	A/C 447			1,163

Being revenue items incorrectly
charged to capital account.

(Inv. 2931	£386)
(Inv. 1090	£600)
(Inv. 212	£177)

			£	£
Dr. Plant and machinery	A/C 447		1,122	
Repairs and renewals	A/C 550			1,122

Being capital item incorrectly
charged to revenue account.
(Moorheat Ltd. 2/12/85—£1,122)

			£	£
Dr. Plant and machinery—depreciation			19	
Plant and machinery—				
Acc. depreciation	A/C 447A			19

Being depreciation undercharged on
capital item incorrectly expensed
(Moorheat Ltd. 2/12/85—£1,122)

	£	£

Dr. Plant and machinery—
        Acc. depreciation   A/C 447A   101
        Plant and machinery—Depreciation   101

Being depreciation overcharged on revenue items
incorrectly capitalised.

(Inv. 2931   £6)
(Inv. 1090   60)
(Inv. 212   35)

Dr. Plant and machinery—
        Acc. depreciation   A/C 447A   7,293
        Plant and machinery—depreciation   7,293

Being depreciation incorrectly charged on items
purchased 1980 already fully depreciated.

Dr. Repairs and maintenance—motor vehicles   250
        Motor vehicles—cost   A/C 449   250

Being revenue item incorrectly capitalised
(Inv. 150   £250)

Dr. Motor vehicles—
        Acc. depreciation   A/C 449A   63
        Motor vehicles—depreciation   63

Being depreciation incorrectly charged on wrong
capital item.
(Inv. 150   £250—depreciation £63)

SUMMARY OF FIXED PHYSICAL ASSETS

Client: *Rebel (Great Britain) Limited*

Year end: *December 28, 1985*

	ASSET CATEGORY			
	FREEHOLD	SHORT LEASEHOLD	PLANT AND MACHINERY	MOTOR VEHICLES
COST OR VALUATION	* Cost/ Valuation in	* Cost/ Valuation in	* Cost/ Valuation in	* Cost/ Valuation in ...
Opening balance	94,921	5,882	178,314	29,717
Additions H3		1,128	85,983	14,114
Revaluation surplus M2				
Capitalised cost leases at 30/12/84			56,145	
	94,921	7,010	320,442	43,831
Government grants H3				
A Disposals		(590)	(7,428)	(13,766)
Closing balance	94,921	6,420	313,014	30,065
DEPRECIATION	4% Cost/ * WDV	various % Cost/ * WDV	20% Cost/ * WDV	25% Cost/ * WDV
Opening balance	14,638	885	129,534	9,627
Revenue charge	1,812	1,904	35,262	9,097
			7,019	
Provision on capitalised leases at 30/12/84	16,450	2,789	169,815	18,724
B Disposals H4		(590)	(6,929)	(8,571)
Closing balance	16,450	2,199	162,886	10,153
NET BOOK AMOUNT				
Closing balance	78,471	4,221	150,128	19,912
Opening balance	80,283	4,997	99,906	20,090
DISPOSALS H4				
A Cost or valuation		590	7,428	13,766
B Aggregate depreciation		590	6,929	8,571
			499	5,195
Less: Revaluation surplus				
Less: Government grants **				
			499	5,195
Proceeds			549	6,600
Surplus (deficit)			50	1,405
VERIFICATION Indicate the extent of: (a) physical verification				
(b) checks on additions and				
(c) checks on disposals Attach details on a separate sheet and cross reference thereto.				

CONCLUSIONS	COMMENTS
1. Have material additions and disposals been checked? 2. What is the basis used for calculating depreciation? Is the asset life on which depreciation is calculated reasonable? 3. Does the balance sheet fairly state fixed physical assets?	

Prepared by: A. Senior

Reviewed by:

Schedule H2

Date: 28/2/86

Date:

* Cost/ Valuation in	* Cost/ Valuation in	* Cost/ Valuation in	TOTAL COST OR VALUATION	* Delete as appropriate. If items are carried at valuation, year of valuation should be given and, if revalued during the year, details should be filed under H7.
			308, 834	
			101, 225	
			56, 145	
			466, 204	
			(21, 784)	
			444, 420	

% Cost/ * WDV	% Cost/ * WDV	% Cost/ * WDV	TOTAL DEPRECIATION	
			152, 684	
			48, 075	
			7, 019	
			207, 778	
			(16, 090)	
			191, 688	

			TOTAL NET BOOK AMOUNT	
			252, 732	
			205, 276	

			TOTALS	
			21, 784	
			16, 090	
			5, 694	
			5, 694	** To be used where Government grants have been taken to a deferred credit account.
			7, 149	
			1, 455	

per ....

FIXED PHYSICAL ASSETS (ADDITIONS)

Schedule H3

Client: Rebel (Great Britain) Ltd Prepared by: A. Senior Date: 28/2/

Year end: December 28, 1985 Reviewed by: Date:

Date acquired	Description of asset	New (N) or Used (S.H.)	Capital payments in year (if on H.P.)	Total cost	Government grants
	SHORT LEASEHOLD LAND AND BUILDINGS				
5/1/85	Warehouse accommodation	leased		1128	
	PLANT AND EQUIPMENT				
	CAPITALISED LEASES				
15/1/85	Leases acquired	−	−	81193	
	PLANT AND MACHINERY				
23/7/85	Casts Ltd − Mould-Plane 348			542	
23/7/85	Casts Ltd − Mould Plane 381			810	
10/10/85	Perry & Sons − Processor Head			625	
10/10/85	Perry & Sons − Processor Case			955	
12/10/85	Gardright Ltd − Machine Guard			736	
2/12/85	Moorheat Ltd − Extrusion heating machine			1122	
				4790	
	MOTOR VEHICLES				
	Autosales Ltd − Rover XLN 637			2907	
	Autosales Ltd − Audi XLP 446			3954	
	Autosales Ltd − Escort XGA 736			1582	
	Chester Perry Ltd − Escort KRM 248			1791	
	Chester Perry Ltd − Granada XJT 903			3880	
				14114	
				101,225	
				H2	H2

COMMENTS

FIXED PHYSICAL ASSETS (SALES & DISPOSALS)　　Schedule H4

Client: Rebel (Great Britain) Ltd　Prepared by: A. Senior　Date: 28/2/86

Year end: December 28, 1985　Reviewed by:　Date:

Date acquired	Description of asset	Cost or valuation	Aggregate depreciation	Revaluation surplus (M2)/ Govt. grants*	Net book value	Proceeds of disposal
	SHORT LEASEHOLD					
15/6/81	Warehouse outbuilding	590	590		–	–
	PLANT AND MACHINERY					
15/1/80	Mixing machine	6000	6000		–	–
16/7/83	Grinder	1000	501		499	549
10/3/79	Mould	428	428		–	–
		7428	6929		499	549
	MOTOR VEHICLES					
29/1/81	2 Rovers COD73	1925	1925		–	500
29/1/81	COD74	1925	1925		–	500
16/7/83	1 Transit BAC 347	1777	1110		667	450
19/7/83	2 Cortinas BDC 942	2250	1218		1032	1000
19/7/83	BDC 943	2250	1219		1031	1050
19/12/83	1 Triumph KLM261	1800	488		1312	1500
12/7/84	1 Granada KVM839	1839	686		1153	1600
		13766	8571		5195	6600
	H2	21784	16090		5694	7149
						5694

Surplus (deficit) on disposal　　1455

*Where Government grants have been taken to a deferred credit account, the amount released on sale or disposal should be recorded in this column.　　H2

COMMENTS

D (3) - SUPER ENGINEERS LIMITED: AUDIT OF STOCKS

Possible Approach to the Assignments

Note: *Limitations necessarily imposed by the presentation of essentially practical material in book form diminish the effectiveness of case studies such as this, to the extent that no direct questioning of members of the client's staff or audit staff is possible. Consequently the inevitable follow-up questions and requests for evidence to support the client's statements cannot be dealt with here. The following approach to the assignments covers in each case the initial requirement together with, where appropriate, possible lines of thought on problems that might arise.*

(a) Physical Existence

Assignments (i), (ii) and (iii) take place in time before the physical inventory and must be covered by the auditor so that he can form an opinion of the adequacy of the instructions and the client's system. Having formed this opinion he may then have recommendations for improving the suggested procedures to put to the client and he will be in a position to decide what particular areas should be covered by his staff at their attendance at the count in addition to satisfying himself that the instructions and systems are complied with. Specific instructions should be given to the staff attending the count and they should be required to write a report. Assignment (iv) relates to the report on the count prepared by the audit staff. In practice the report for the audit manager would summarise the reports of those attending the count and draw conclusions regarding its accuracy and acceptability. However in view of the limitations outlined above it is proposed to deal with all the assignments in the form of one report to the audit manager:

Report

(i) The stocktaking questionnaire, completed as far as possible from reading the company's instructions, is attached to this report.

(ii) The following information is still required (numbers at left are references to questionnaire):

Preparation for inventory counting

(4) Will the instructions be discussed with the staff to ensure that they are understood? Although staff involved are required to be familiar with the instructions (General 6), the auditor should ascertain how this is to be ensured, the extent of the discussions and the seniority of the officials involved.

(5) Will stocks be arranged so that counting is simplified? The instructions are not clear or sufficiently detailed on this point, maybe because stocks are well stacked and segregated anyway. However the auditor must satisfy himself and should make a pre-count inspection of all locations.

(7) Is there an organisation chart for the count indicating responsibilities? The auditor, let alone the client's staff involved, should know, before the count starts, the chain of responsibility and the allocation of duties. The list provided to the cost office does not seem adequate for this purpose.

(8) There is no indication that arrangements have been made to shut down production and prohibit movements. In fact production is probably to continue and consequently the auditor must ensure in advance that the arrangements to deal with cut-off are adequate.

(9) Will stocks be precounted and sealed where possible? There are apparently no written instructions; however those actually involved may be intending to do some precounting—this should be established.

(11) Lists or plans of stock locations are not circularised with the instructions. However they may be available from the department concerned.

(12) The instructions do not require visits by senior officials to ensure compliance, and enquiries should be made of the officials concerned as to the extent of supervision they intend to exercise.

Cut-off arrangements

The instructions do not go into detail on cut-off arrangements. Answers must be obtained verbally from the appropriate officials and staff to the questions in the questionnaire in advance of the count.

Counting and measuring procedures

In this case also the instructions are not sufficiently detailed for the auditor to be sure that adequate procedures have been set up and he should question the individuals concerned as to what they intend to do and inspect the stores himself to see whether inventory is satisfactorily identified, etc.

(iii) Certain important weaknesses in the stocktaking procedures are apparent from the instructions themselves:

(a) Implication of cut-off problems not adequately covered by detailed instructions. Movements during the count should be kept to a minimum and must be adequately controlled.

(b) Pre-numbered tear off tags not to be used. Their use would be a much more effective guarantee against omissions and double counting than the safeguards in the system proposed.
If the further questions in (ii) above received negative answers, the following would be particularly serious weaknesses in addition to (a) and (b) above.

63

(1) Preparation for inventory counting

(a) There would be no requirement for all locations to be visited by senior officials prior to and during the count to ensure compliance with the instructions. General instructions refer to the general responsibility of executives over their departments but do not detail their responsibilities over the count itself and do not set out particular procedures to be followed by them. This would be a serious weakness particularly if the actual count were supervised by the storekeeper himself.

(b) There would be no plan or list of locations. Such a plan or list would be useful to both company and auditors to ensure that the count covered all locations. The existence of a location problem is indicated by the departmental instructions. (Paragraph 5.)

(2) Cut-off arrangements

The instructions would contain no reference to goods held for others or goods held at outside locations. If there are such goods it is a major weakness that the instructions do not deal with procedure to be followed. Goods held for others are not the company's stock and a separate system of documentation and records should be maintained. Goods at outside locations should be incorporated into the count and similar count procedures should be followed.

(3) Counting and measuring procedures

(a) If the inventory supervisor were the storekeeper this may be a major weakness since the physical count would not therefore exercise any independent control over the storekeeper. Misappropriation of stock or known errors could be concealed by the storekeeper.

(b) Instructions do not adequately cover the physical identification of obsolete, surplus or defective stocks. No indication is given as to how stock is identified or who is responsible—a major weakness. An accurate valuation depends on the correct assessment at the time of the physical count of the condition of the stock.

(iv) The report prepared by the audit staff is clearly not adequate.

This situation would not necessarily be entirely the fault of the staff attending the count but may be the result of inadequate briefing by the senior auditor. The following further information would be needed and the answers should have been contained in the report:

(a) Were the company's instructions followed in all respects?
(b) How did you satisfy yourself that all locations were covered by the company's count?
(c) How did you satisfy yourself that obsolete, surplus, or defective stock was satisfactorily dealt with and separately recorded? Did you count any?
(d) Was the stock neatly stored and was the count made systematically?
(e) Were there any movements of stock during the count?

(f) Were the test counts performed by audit staff carried out by checking items counted to stock sheets and vice versa?

(g) Did you discuss differences found on our own test checks with the supervisor and establish satisfactory reasons for the differences?

(h) Did you satisfy yourself that all cards had been collected and accounted for after the count?

Preparation for inventory counting	*Yes or No*	*Cross reference to paragraphs in inventory instructions*
(1) Are there written stocktaking instructions?	Yes	General and Departmental instructions
(2) Will all staff sign to indicate completion of the work for which they are responsible?	Yes	General 12b Departmental 8
(3) Are there separate written instructions for each grade of staff?	No	But assistants must have access to instructions (General 6)
(4) If there are written instructions, will these be discussed with staff to ensure that they are understood?	?	General 8 lays down a general requirement re tidiness, but Departmental 5 suggests possible location problems
(5) Will stocks be arranged so that counting is simplified? (a) In regular sized stacks/bundles (b) Like items in the same place (c) In areas which are properly segregated	?	General, 5, 6 and 7 Departmental 1
(6) Are there adequate staffing arrangements?	Yes	General 6
(7) Is there an organisation chart for the count indicating responsibilities?	?	Departmental 1
(8) Have arrangements been made to shut down production and prohibit movement of stocks?	No	Departmental 2, 3, 12, 13, 14 suggest cut-off problems
(9) Will stocks be precounted and sealed where possible?	?	General 11 may be relevant
(10) Will stocks of partially completed items be reduced to a minimum?	N/A	Not applicable to this department
(11) Is there a list/plan of all stock locations?	?	
(12) Will all locations be visited by senior officials prior to and during the count to ensure compliance with instructions?	?	General 7 indicated no requirement for this

Preparation for inventory counting	Yes or No	Cross reference to paragraphs in inventory instructions
Cut-off arrangements		
(1) Will goods arriving from suppliers during the count be properly segregated?	?	Are all finished goods stocks ex w.i.p.?
(2) Are there pre-numbered documents recording:		
(a) Goods received	?	
(b) Goods despatched	?	Departmental 12, 13
(c) Internal transfers	?	Departmental 3
(3) Have arrangements been made to record final pre-count numbers for each document under (2)?	?	
(4) Are there adequate procedures to ensure that the books of account match the physical movement (indicated by the documents in (2))?	?	General 4 gives general requirement
(5) Will all goods held for others be excluded from the count e.g. by use of 'Do not inventory' tags?	?	
(6) Will all goods held at outside locations be included?	?	
(7) Is the method used for accruing 'pre-inventory' purchases satisfactory?	?	
Will these accruals be separately recorded to enable subsequent charges to be matched against them?	?	
Counting and measuring procedures		
(1) Generally are the arrangements for counting such that all inventory owned will be counted accurately and quickly?	Yes	Departmental 8 and 9
(2) Are there safeguards against:		
(a) double counting	Yes	Departmental 8 and 9
(b) omissions		
(3) Will pre-numbered tear-off count tags be used?	No	Departmental 8 and 9
(4) Will records of the first count be removed prior to re-checks?	No	Departmental 8 and 9
(5) Will records of count be written indelibly in ink or biro?	Yes	Departmental 6
(6) Is inventory identified satisfactorily (e.g. by permanent markings on bins, floor areas, etc.)?	?	

Preparation for inventory counting	Yes or No	Cross reference to paragraphs in inventory instructions
(7) Will the persons counting be independent of those responsible for the stock?	?	
(8) Have arrangements been made to acquire for hire 'conversion' scales for counting large quantities of small items?	?	
(9) Have all measuring devices (scales, meters, etc.) been tested *recently* for accuracy)?	?	
(10) Have arrangements been made to obtain written confirmation of all stocks held by third parties or on sale or return?	?	
11) Are methods of identifying: (a) obsolete (b) surplus (c) defective stocks satisfactory?	?	Departmental 10 may refer to this

(b) Excess and Slow Moving Stocks

Report to audit manager

(1) The following additional information is required from the client to enable an assessment of the provisions for excess and slow moving stocks to be made:

(a) production plans
(b) future sales trends and forecasts
(c) contracts
(d) current order position
(e) loss of large customers
(f) changes in specification
(g) competition
(h) sales in year under review and in previous year analysed by product lines in months and corresponding budgets
(i) comparative figures
(j) life span of products

(2) The company's previous provisions for excess and slow moving stocks should be reviewed to assess the realism of the company's past judgment.

(3) The stock turnover ratios should be calculated and reviewed.

(4) The above information will be used to assess whether the stock in hand at 31st December is saleable within a reasonable period and whether the provision arrived at by the two year method is sufficiently accurate.

(c) Valuation

Report to audit manager

(1) Variances are applied to the stock valuation as follows:
The client calculates how many months' purchases or production give rise to an amount equal to the value of materials, labour and overheads in raw material stocks, work-in-progress and finished goods.

(2) This method assumes that physical movement is on a FIFO basis. The fact of this must be established. It would be appropriate to deal separately with materials which may be stock-piled and/or may not come within the normal production cycle.

(3) It should be ascertained whether or not standards are frequently reviewed. If standard costs are used for stock valuation then they should bear a reasonable relationship to the actual costs obtaining in the period (see Appendix 1 to Statement of Standard Accounting Practice No. 9 on 'Stocks and Work in Progress').

(4) The labour performance variance has not been applied presumably on the grounds that it has arisen through inefficiency or undercapacity (although the overhead variance has been applied).

(5) The labour performance and overhead variances are large and explanations and analysis would be required before it would be possible to form an opinion on their treatment in relation to the stock valuation. In particular, enquiries should be directed towards the relationship between these two variances, and the reasons for an increasingly favourable overhead variance when the schedule of production movements seems to indicate an increasing under-recovery.

(6) Information is required also on the basis on which the standards were set up. If they are not based on a criterion of normal capacity and normal production the resulting variances may be misleading.

(7) The method adopted is a reasonable and acceptable attempt to apply variances to the valuation. In this particular case an error has been made in arithmetic on Document (8) Application of Variances. The amount of £911 carried down as the total variance on materials and labour in work-in-progress should be a credit.

(8) There is an error in the valuation of service type unit A on the Stock Sheet. The amount should be £14,354, not £28,707. Enquiries would have to be made to ascertain the reasons for the error and the internal control weaknesses which not only permitted the error but caused it not to be detected. If the amount of £28,707 is incorrect this will naturally affect the variance calculation.

D (4) - THE NATIONAL FOOD CO. (U.K.) LIMITED: AUDIT OF CASH AND BANK

Adequacy of Work Programmed for Audit of Cash

Company Procedures:

From an evaluation of current Company procedures for cash the following strengths and weaknesses were noted:

Strengths:

(1) There is good segregation of duties as between cashier section which is within the Secretarial Department and the Accounts Department. The possibility of collusion between cashier and ledger clerks is therefore diminished.

(2) All cheques require two signatures of responsible officials to make a valid payment.

(3) Bank accounts are reconciled monthly and reviewed by the Chief Accountant, an official unconnected with the cash function.

(4) All paid invoices are cancelled with a stamp to prevent resubmission for duplicate payment. Note however that weakness number (4) effectively negates this strength.

(5) Brussels branch bank account is maintained on an imprest basis making it easy for Head Office management to control the expenditure.

(6) All employees are covered by fidelity bond insurance to cover the company for loss from fraudulent conversion.

(7) All bank accounts must be authorised by the Board of Directors.

(8) Cash and cheque receipts are banked daily.

(9) Sales ledger cash and cheques are tightly controlled and checked (i.e. as part of the monthly control account reconciliation procedures, receipts per the sales ledger are agreed to the total month's receipts as recorded by the cashier's department).

(10) No cheques payable to bearer or to cash are allowed, except for petty cash.

(11) Cheques are supported by back up documentation at the time of signing.

(12) Cheques, after signing are *not* returned to the preparers, but are immediately despatched.

(13) Spoilt cheques are cancelled and are closely controlled.

Weaknesses:

(1) There is no control over mail opening or pre-listing of cheques and cash received by the mail room. Tape lists are made by the cashier and accounts clerk.

(2) The Company cashes employees' cheques so leaving more room for manipulation of funds.

(3) The Manager-Secretarial has access to cheques after signature and also passes them for payment.

(4) As the invoices are stamped PAID and dated before the cheque signatories see them they could still be presented for payment while the date remains current or alternatively the clerk might deliberately not cancel invoices so as to allow fraudulent resubmission.

(5) No restrictive endorsement is made on cheques received to prevent endorsement to a third party.

Evaluation of scope and conclusion

The Company's procedures are basically strong, relying on segregation of functions, approvals and counter signatures; the weaknesses noted do not negate these strengths.

In my opinion the programme as drawn up is adequate to fulfil the objectives of this section of the audit.

C. H. HERE
October 30, 1981

Senior   S. P. VISION   November 1, 1981.
Manager JOHN ERNEST November 5, 1981.

NATIONAL FOOD CO. (UK) LIMITED AUDIT DEC 31, 1981

SUGGESTIONS FOR IMPROVEMENTS IN COMPANY PROCEDURES

(1) Although it is Company procedure to run the Brussels branch account on an imprest basis, at December 31 the balance was in excess of the imprest. We recommend that to retain the control features the imprest level must be set and maintained.

(2) As the Brussels branch office increases in size attempts should be made to segregate the cashier function from any other accounting function.

(3) We recommend that all sales ledger receipts should be received direct at Head Office, reducing the delay in crediting funds to the overdraft account, and centralising responsibility for major cash receipts.

(4) Mail opening and the immediate listing and restrictive endorsement of cheques should be given higher priority and be the responsibility of an officer of the Company.

(5) Invoices should be cancelled by PAID stamp by the second signatory to the cheque paying the liability, to ensure that no invoices are paid twice.

A-1

The National Food Co. (U.K.) Ltd.
Bank Reconciliations
Audit Dec 31. 81.

C. H. Here
Feb. 5. 82.

	X-ref.	THE REGIONAL BANK CURRENT	THE REGIONAL BANK DEPOSIT	THE NEXT BANK OF BRUSSELS CURRENT
Balance per bank statement - December 31 1981	A-1 / 1	(85,502·19) ✗	NIL	488·19 ✗
Outstanding cheques	A-1 / 2	(30,857·77)	-	(2,031·53)
Deposits in transit	A-1 / 2	1,853·42	-	1,532·32
Other items		5,225·00 ①	-	-
Balance per books - December 31, 1981		£ (109,281·54)	NIL	£ (11·02)
		A	A	A

① Adjusting journal entry - overdraft interest not accrued in books

Dr.	Selling, General + Administration Expense	5,225·00	
Cr.	Bank Overdraft		5,225·00

Receipt for Bank Statements and Cancelled Cheques

I received intact from a representative of Steinbeck Hemmingway + Co. on Feb. 5. 72 the following listed bank statements and related cancelled cheques.

The Regional Bank   Current A/c. Jan. 1. 82 - Jan 10 82
Next Bank of Brussels Current A/c Jan. 1. 82 - Jan 10 82

Peter Thompson
PETER THOMPSON - CASHIER.

✗ - Agreed to cut off bank statement received direct Jan 1. 82 and company bank statement at Dec. 31. 81.

T - Totalled

71

A

C. A. Kane

Feb. 5. 82.

The National Food Co. (U.K.) Ltd.

Cash.

Audit Dec. 31. 81.

					X - ref.	as adjusted Dec. 31. 80	per books Dec. 31. 81
The Regional Bank Ltd.	–	Current	a/c.			3,221.98 ✗	(109,281 54) √
	–	Deposit	a/c.	A-1		111,000.00 ✗	–
The Next Bank of Brussels	–	Branch	a/c.			2,501.20 ✗	(11.02) √
Petty Cash.						400.00 ✗	500.00 ②
						116,123.18	(108,792 56)
						TB - A	TB - A
Bank overdraft	– Secured					–	–

① Reclassifying Journal Entry – Overdraft

	Dr.	Cash					114,506.54
	Cr	Overdraft					114,506.54

② No work done because of the inactive nature of the account and the low through put.

③ See inter-bank transfer schedule   A-1 ④/4

④ See bank reconciliation schedule   A-1 ⑤

✗ – Agreed to audit work papers for year ended Dec. 31. 80.

√ – Agreed to cash books and general ledger.

adjustments		as adjusted	reclassifications		as adjusted and reclassified.	
Dr.	Cr.	Dec. 31. 81	Dr.	Cr.	Dec. 31. 81	
	(5,225·00) ④	(114,506·54)	114,506·54 ①		–	
		–			–	
511·82 ③		500·80			500·80	
		500·00			500·00	
511·82	(5,225·00)	(113,505·74)	114,506·54	–	1,000·80	TT
		TB - A			TB - A	
				114,506·54 ①	114,506·54	TT
					TB - L.	

NOTES :- (i) Change in cash position was due to £150,000 overdraft facility made available by Regional Bank for extension of factory.

(ii) Overdraft secured by floating charge on assets, $\frac{A-1}{1}$

CONCLUSION :- In my opinion the cash balances are properly classified in the accounts and properly represent cash on hand, in transit or at banks, and all restrictions on funds are properly disclosed.

Chris H. Here

Feb. 5. 82.

T - Totalled.

TT - Cross totalled.

73

The National Food Co. (U.K.) Ltd.
Bank Replies
Audit   Dec. 31. 81.

C. H. Hene
Feb. 5. 82

THE REGIONAL BANK LIMITED.

Exchange Buildings

High Street, London, E.C.2.

TELEPHONE 01 999 1010 . TELEX 238211 . CABLE ADDRESS— Regban LONDON, E.C.2.

Steinbeck, Hemingway & Co.,
Saint House,
92, Fore Street,
London, E.C.2.   January 12, 1982

Dear Sirs,

                    Re: National Food Company (U.K.) Ltd

        In accordance with your request of December 15, 1981 we are
pleased to confirm the following information as outstanding on our
books as of close of business on December 31, 1981 for the
above named firm.

    1. Current Account (A/C No. 632475) - £35,502.19 Debit.⎫ A-1
        Deposit Account (A/C No. 356213) - NIL.   ⎬
    2. None.
    3. Overdraft interest accrued not debited NIL.
    4. See bank statement.
    5. None.
    6. Overdraft facility of £150,000 granted.
    7. Floating charge on assets held as security for   A
        overdraft - limited to £150,000.
    8. None.
    9. None.

        We also enclose statement of account, together with the
relevant cheques covering period January 1 to 10, 1982.

        No other items were outstanding on our books as of your
audit date.

                        Yours faithfully,

                        Alan J. Hart

                        Alan J. Hart
                        Manager

74

The National Food Co. (U.K.) Ltd.
Bank Replies
Audit Dec. 31. 81.

C. H. Here
Feb. 5. 82

THE NEXT BANK OF BRUSSELS
94, Rue du Trône, Brussels 15.

TELEPHONE 6211 NATIONAL.

In replying please quote initials.
AUD/CONTROL.

Steinbeck, Hemingway & Co.
Saint House,
92, Fore Street,
London E.C.2.

January 13, 1982

Re: National Food Company (U.K.) Ltd
As of December 31, 1981

We hereby certify that our records showed that the
following outstandings for account of the above on the date
indicated:-

Balance of Account(s) (No.43216) - Belgian Francs 58,582.80
            Credit @ 120 = £488.19 E   A-1
Accounts Closed - None
Overdraft Interest - £NIL
Set-off - None
Overdraft Facility - None
Security - None
Contingent Liabilities - None

Miscellaneous There were two cheques paid in the period
January 1, 1982-January 10, 1982 in excess
of Fr. 30,000.
Air Freight - Travel International Ltd
  December 20, 1981 005435 Fr. 46,704.00 ①   A-1
Regional Bank Ltd   2
  December 30, 1981 055440 Fr. 183,878.40 ②

① @ 120 = £ 389.20 E
② @ 120 = £1,532.32 E

Reference Your letter of December 15, 1981

D. Gilbert

c.c.National Food Company (U.K.) Ltd.   D. Gilbert
Enc.   Authorised
YC   Signature

E - Calculation checked

$\frac{A-1}{2}$

The National Food Co. (U.K.) Ltd.

Outstanding cheques and deposits in transit

C.H.Here
5.2.82

Audit 31. 12. 81

Source :- Company prepared reconciliation.
Scope :- Amounts over £250.

Regional Bank - Outstanding Cheques.

Date	Cheque No.	Amount.	
²/₁₁	368	605·67 √	①
³/₁₂	522	258·90 √	①
⁸/₁₂	523	35·10	
²⁷/₁₂ {	630	427·81 √	
	631	1,081·90 √	
	632	325·70 √	
²⁸/₁₂ {	633	3,218·60 √	
	634	20,000·00 √	
	635	128·35	
²⁹/₁₂ {	636	231·87	①
	637	2·89	
	638	98·61	①
³⁰/₁₂ {	639	2·81	
	640	4·99	
	641	321·94 √	
	643	1,481·36 √	
	644	33·51	①
	645	243·21	
³¹/₁₂ {	646	896·41 √	
	647	305·46 √	
	648	345·02 √	
	649	788·66 √	
		30,857·77 A-1 *	

Next Bank - Outstanding cheques

			*
²⁰/₁₂	438	389·20 √	②
²⁷/₁₂	439	110·01	
³⁰/₁₂	440 $\frac{A-1}{4}$	1,532·32 √	②
		2,031·53 A-1 *	

Regional Bank - Deposits in transit

			*	Date deposited per bank
³⁰/₁₂	$\frac{A-1}{4}$	1,532·32	③	⁷/₁ √
³¹/₁₂		300·00		³/₁ √
		21·10		
		1,853·42 A-1 *		

Next Bank - Deposits in transit

			*	
³⁰/₁₂	$\frac{A-1}{4}$	1,532·32	③	⁴/₁ √
		1,532·32 A-1 *		

① Listed as exceptions $\frac{A-1}{3}$

② No returned cheque but items agreed to bank letters on $\frac{A-1}{1}$ for date, payee number and amount.

③ Sales receipts received in Brussels being transferred to Head Office.

Note :-

(i) Cheques dated after year end were examined. The date of the bank endorsement did not precede the audit date and all of these appeared on the list of outstanding cheques at 12.31.81.

(ii) Working from the cash book - all payment from December 16 to 31 were accounted for as clearing bank before 12.31.81 or appearing on lists of outstanding cheques attached.

√ - Traced to cash disbursement record as to number date, amount and payee. All cleared the bank during the period Jan.1 to 10, 1982. There were no unusual endorsements. All signatories were authorised.

√ᵛ - Agreed to cash receipts book.

√ - Traced to bank statement received direct.

T - Totalled.

The National Food Co (U.K.) Ltd.
Schedule of Exceptions
Audit Dec. 31. 81

A-1

3

C.H. Hene
Feb · 5 · 82

Source: Cash Book
& Reconciliation

Cheque Number	Bank			Payee		
03 68	Regional			D. A. Bloom Ltd.		
05 22	Regional			Copying Equipment Rentals		
06 38	Regional			Andrew George		
06 36	Regional			G. E. Roberts		
06 44	Regional			J. O. Anderson		

Amount	Reason for exception	Explanation & disposition
605.67	long outstanding cheque drawn Nov. 12. 81	cleared in cut off period
258.90	long outstanding cheque drawn Dec. 3. 81	
98.61	Employee cheques	all three are members of sales force traced to December 1981 expense Report.
231.87		
33.51		

CONCLUSION:—

In my opinion there were no exceptional payments made which were not satisfactorily explained by the company.

Chris. H. Hare
Feb. 5. 82

The National Food Co. (U.K.) Ltd.
Schedule of Adjustments
Audit Dec. 31·81

C. H Hann
Feb. 5. 82.

Schedule	Description of Adjustment.	Dr.	Cr.	Disposition
A	Reclassification of overdraft to short term liabilities			
	Cash	114,506·54		
	Bank Overdraft		114,506 54	Reclassify JE 2/82
A-1	Adjusting journal entry re bank interest not accrued.			
	Selling, General and Administration expense	5,225·00		
	Bank Overdraft		5,225·00	Adjust JE 2/82
A-1 / 4	Adjusting journal entry re cheque not retained by branch			
	Cash	511·82		
	Head Office Account		511·82	Adjust JE 2/82

A-1
/4

The National Food Co. (U.K.) Ltd.
Inter- and Intra- Bank Transfers

Scope: Dec 20-Jan 10.
Source: Cash Book.   Audit Dec. 31. 86

C. H. Hen
Feb. 5. 8

Date Withdrawn		Date Deposited		Cheque Number	Regional	Bank
Per Books	Per Banks	Per Books	Per Banks		Current	Deposit
Dec 27.81	Dec 31. 81	Dec 27 81	Dec.31. 81	0626	8,501·72 (8,501·72)	-
Dec 27 81	Dec 31 81		①	0628	511·82	-
Dec 30. 81	(Jan 4. 82)	Dec 30. 81	(Jan 7. 82)	440	(1,532·32)	-
(Jan 10. 82)	(Jan 10. 82)	(Jan 10. 82)	(Jan 10. 82)	-	1,000·00	-
	① No deposit in transit recorded. On investigation the Bank					
	agrees that it was credited to another account by mistake :-					
	A.J.E. raised :					
	Dr.	Cash			511·82	
	Cr.	Head Office account			511·82	

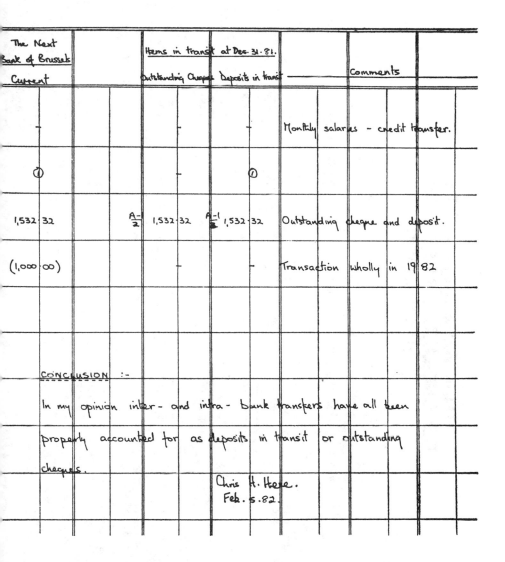

The Next Bank of Brussels Current			Items in transit at Dec. 31. 81.				Comments		
			Outstanding Cheques	Deposits in transit					
-			-	-			Monthly salaries - credit transfer.		
①			-	①					
1,532·32		$\frac{A-1}{2}$	1,532·32	$\frac{A-1}{2}$ 1,532·32			Outstanding cheque and deposit.		
(1,000·00)			-	-			Transaction wholly in 1982		
CONCLUSION :-									
In my opinion inter- and intra- bank transfers have all been									
properly accounted for as deposits in transit or outstanding									
cheques.									
				Chris H. Here. Feb. 5.82.					

D (5) - REBEL (G.B.) LIMITED: RECONCILIATIONS OF CREDITORS' STATEMENTS

	Buckley & Co Ltd £	Canam Chemical Supply Ltd £	Brighter Fabriks Ltd £	Fauril Industries Ltd £
Balance per purchase ledger 28.12.85	8,478.60	6,947.20	2,387.45	4,956.00
Add: Invoices/(Credits) in statements not in ledger		356.85 (31.12.85)	429.11 (30.12.85) 303.21 (31.12.85)	1,250.00 (29.12.85)
	8,478.60	7,304.05	3,119.77	6,206.00
Add: Cash in transit at 31.12.85	12,000.00 (27.12.85)		1,363.44 (31.12.85)	5,683.26 (31.12.85)
	20,478.60	7,304.05	4,483.21	11,889.26
Less: (Invoices)/Credits in ledger not statement	–	–	–	–
	20,478.60	7,304.05	4,483.21	11,889.26
Add/(Deduct): Other errors.				
Discount taken by Rebel not allowed by Supplier – 31.5.85 and 5.12.85	320.00			
Error in calculating discount taken by Rebel – 30.11.85	100.00		7.14	
Posting error in invoice of 16.12.85 – £2,593.80 entered as £2,953.80		(360.00)		
Posting error in invoice of 4.12.85 – £1,347.91 entered as £1,437.91			(90.00)	

	Buckley & Co Ltd £	Canam Chemical Supply Ltd £	Brighter Fabriks Ltd £	Fauril Industries Ltd £
Posting error in invoice of 4.12.85 – £245.30 entered as £254.30			(9.00)	
Credit note entered as an invoice 6.12.85 – £63.20 doubled up			(126.40)	
	20,898.60	6,944.05	4,264.95	11,889.26
Unidentified differences	–	98.23	–	–
Balance per statement	20,898.60	7,042.28	4,264.95	11,889.26
			(see Note 5)	

Further steps to be taken:

1. *Invoices/(Credits) in statements not in ledger*
   (a) Examine if these invoices or credits can be located.
   (b) Ascertain the date of delivery of the goods and if prior to 31.12.85 provide for these items.

2. *Cash in transit at 31.12.85*
   (a) Examine cancelled cheque and ensure it is dated December 1985 and has been presented to your client's bank in 1986.
   (b) Ascertain whether these cheques were mailed in 1985. If mailed in 1986 the amount should be added back to creditors by adjusting the bank balance.

3. *(Invoices)/Credits in ledger not in statements*
   Examine and ascertain why these do not appear in the statements. (In this example this particular step does not apply).

4. *Unidentified differences*
   Write or telephone Canam requesting a statement after obtaining the client's permission. This amount may be considered immaterial and the client may be willing to provide for it without further investigation or indeed no further enquiries may be considered necessary.

5. *Brighter Fabriks statement* shows a balance of £4,155.05. This must be adjusted for addition errors on 2.12.85 (£10), 12.12.85 (10p) and 14.12.85 (£100) (Net £109.90) to give a final total of £4,264.95.

83

D (6) - TRAIN LIMITED: ANALYTICAL REVIEW OF CREDITORS

(1) Comparison of creditors listings—1989 and 1988.
The 3 main suppliers accounted for £26,844 of the 1989 year-end creditors balance. In 1988 there had not been any purchases in the latter months of that year—see below for reasons.

(2) Average number of days purchases included in year end taken by the creditors company:

1989	1988
$\frac{29,831}{83,005} \times 365 = 131$ days	$\frac{1,139}{25,499} \times 365 = 16$ days

      1989 figures might suggest
(i)   Increased purchasing in latter months of the year
(ii) the company appears to be getting extended credit from its suppliers
(iii) delay in paying creditors due to cash flow problems
(iv) incorrect entries may have been made either through error or to hide defalcations.

(3) *Review of level of purchases*

(a) *1989*—given the relatively large opening stock of finished goods, additional materials would not have been purchased and production would have been curtailed till this stock was depleted. Purchasing was probably stepped up towards the year end—as is reflected in the figure of closing materials stock.

(b) *1988*—the Company's purchasing in the year was low given the large opening stock of materials and the low activity (sales) in the year. As finished goods stock built up towards the end of the year the purchasing activity would have been reduced even further as production was probably curtailed—resulting in the very low level of year-end creditors.

(4) *Period of credit taken by company*

    1 month for both years—as is evident from creditors' aging schedules.

D (7) - C.B.A. COMPANY LIMITED: PROFIT AND LOSS ANALYSIS

(a) Audit Programme

Objectives

To determine whether the profit and loss account reflects the results of the company's operations for the year in accordance with generally accepted accounting principles, and whether it makes adequate disclosure of any unusual items and of any changes in the basis of accounting.

Audit Procedures

(**Note:** *The opinion on this section of the audit will be based to a considerable degree upon the significance for the profit and loss account of evidence collected during previous audit work relating to the balance sheet and the company's accounting procedures.*)

(1) Write brief memorandum listing and explaining all material differences between 1980 results and (a) 1979 results and (b) 1980 budgets; end the memorandum with overall conclusion relating to objectives of this section of the audit. (It will not be possible to complete the memorandum until all the other steps below have been carried out; but the latter should be undertaken primarily to provide material for this memorandum and its conclusion.)

(2) Prepare analysis of sales and gross profit percentages by divisions by months for 1979 and 1980 (or better, obtain a copy of the client's schedules of this data). Obtain and check explanations from company operating staff for material variations between years and between 1980 actual and 1980 budget. (In this and other comparative reviews against 1979, refer first to 1979 audit files to ensure 1979 figures were not themselves unusual in some respect.)

N.B. (i) In the case of the management accounting information for the divisions, review their reconciliation with the financial accounts in order to ascertain the adequacy of the management accounts.

(ii) In the case of the budgets, enquire into the procedures used in their preparations to ascertain whether or not they are likely to be sufficiently reliable for audit purposes.

(3) Check that the system for granting quantity discounts has been adequately reviewed and tested during audit of accounting procedures and internal control.

(4) Obtain client's calculations of royalties payable; check these against current royalty agreements and test against 1980 sales figures.

85

(5) Obtain set of monthly management accounts; review as far as possible at interim audit, complete review at final audit, paying special attention to the accounts for the last month of the year. Obtain explanations for the following, where material:

  (a) monthly material price variances
  (b) monthly material usage variances
  (c) monthly labour variances
  (d) overhead expenditure variances on a cumulative basis
  (e) overhead absorption variances on a cumulative basis.

This work should be carried out in conjunction with audit of the company's stock valuation. Standard cost is not of itself an acceptable basis of stock valuation in annual accounts and should only be accepted as an approximation to actual cost. Consideration should be given (at an interim date if possible) to adjustment of standards, including overhead absorption rates, if these are resulting in substantial cumulative variances.

(6) In the course of audit of stocks, check the write-off of obsolete and deficient stocks and tie-in totals agreed to the profit and loss account.

(7) Tie in expense figures for bad debts and depreciation in profit and loss records to those agreed during balance sheet verification.

(8) Obtain and note explanations for variations from 1979 and from budget (on management accounts) in categories of Selling Expenses and of General and Administrative Expenses. Analyse by months, and if necessary by entry, account headings for which no simple explanation is available for variations.

(9) Review for appropriate accounting and tax treatment charges to the following accounts (noting particularly proper distinction between capital and revenue):

  Repairs (factory, vehicle, administration)
  Professional fees
  Travel and entertainment
  Subscriptions and donations

(For audit purposes examine only material items; smaller items may be examined if requested by the manager responsible for the tax computation.)

(10) Review 'other income/expense'. Note explanations for major variations from previous year. Review appropriateness of classification of items under this general heading. Tie in profit on sale of fixed assets to work on disposals of fixed assets.

(11) Check profit and loss account drafted for publication for compliance with legal requirements and SSAPs. Examine how items of 'other income/expense' have been disclosed or grouped with other accounts.

(12) Review the results of procedural audit tests and of detailed work in connection with debtors, stocks and fixed assets for comments and opinions relevant to the audit of the profit and loss account.

(13) If the client prepares reconciliations of throughput:

(a) Examine the reconciliations in detail, determine whether agreement has been properly made and test with appropriate sources (e.g. summaries of purchase and sales invoices, production records and lists of inventory balances).

(b) Determine whether significant discrepancies have been investigated and adequate explanations obtained.

(b) Possible Errors and Major Changes for Follow-Up

10–1 Veterinary Division
    (a) Sharp drop in sales during last four months of 1980 to a level less than half that of the previous year.
    (b) Gross margins for 1980 12%, down from 30% in 1979.
    (c) Gross margins in May and June 1980 25% and 20% respectively, but for rest of 1980 about 10%.

10–1 Non-Ethical Division
    (a) Why does the gross margin fall on non-ethical sales for September and October 1980?

20–1 Veterinary Division. Enquire into the large 1980 variances.

30–1 'Not-deductible' Travel and Entertainment. Why have these expenses fallen in 1980?

30–1 Selling expenses. Commissions are up by 25% in 1980, but total sales are down by about 3%. Sales mix has changed; check whether commission rates vary between major categories of product.

30–1 Carriage out. Disappears in 1980—presumably reclassified to some other heading, probably within cost of sales.

30–2 Repairs. Very low by comparison with 1979 (but was 1979 the abnormal level and 1980 the normal? Check with 1979 working papers before asking client for explanations).

30–2 Salaries have increased by 8.8% but wages by only 4.2%. Why are these increases different? How do they compare to the present rate of inflation after taking account of staffing levels?

30–2 Professional fees have risen sharply. Why is this? In the case of any fees paid to solicitors ascertain the nature of the fees: these could indicate litigation against the company.

50 Why was no dividend received from the associated company in 1979? Review the accounts of the associated company for the two years to ensure the company has taken up its share of all dividends distributed.

50 Profit on sales of fixed assets. How does this arise?

50 Profit on exchange. Where was this classified in 1979?

50 Rents received. Have these been reclassified in 1980, or have none been received this year? If the latter is the case obtain explanation of changed circumstances.

50 Bank interest expense. What is the reason for the large increase in 1980?

E (1) - PROCESS LIMITED: ASSESSMENT OF GOING CONCERN

1.   The immediate uncertainty relates to whether or not any of the long-term creditors will demand payment and exercise their legal rights to foreclose on the security of their loans.

Another uncertainty arises from the fact that the Company is still in a development stage. It is not yet proven by a track record that there are no critical problems related to supplies, technical aspects of production, personnel, marketing etc. It can be seen that the financing of the Company development went wrong somewhere; either due to undercapitalisation, delayed development, or cost overruns.

These uncertainties relating to the development of the Company have a direct effect on the balance sheet. Fixed assets are being accounted for on a historical cost basis and are classified as non-current as they would be in an operating company. They are so accounted for and presented in an operating company because of the utilisation of the 'going concern concept'. Under this concept day-to-day or even year-to-year changes in the market values of the fixed assets do not affect the accounting for such assets. The objective is to account for their recovery, through depreciation, in the results of the operations.

2.   It would be misleading to use the 'going concern concept' for a company in a development stage without any qualification, if only because the company is not yet a going concern.

A suitable qualification would be '… subject to the recovery of the Company's investment in fixed assets through successful future operations …'.

Going back to the immediate uncertainty of the overdue long-term loans we see that, should any of the creditors demand their overdue loans, this would most probably have the effect of putting the Company into liquidation. This would mean that the going concern concept would no longer be operative and a number of adjustments would have to be made to the balance sheet, as will be discussed below, which are so substantial and fundamental that any type of opinion or qualification would not be appropriate. In this case a disclaimer along the following lines might be appropriate in the audit report:

> 'In view of the significance of the matter discussed in the preceding paragraph, we are unable to express, and we do not express, an opinion on the accounts referred to above'.

One way of resolving the uncertainties would be to ask the Company to obtain formal waivers from each creditor bank stating that they will not foreclose on their securities for the amounts of the overdue loans.

In the longer term, it appears that the Company has to come to an arrangement with the long-term creditors for a rescheduling of the loans.

3.   The first adjustment relates to the fact that the long-term debt is no longer long-term and it should be classified as current.

This means that the Company is going into liquidation and the following economic facts have to be recognised as we move from utilising the 'going concern concept' to 'liquidation values'. The more important of the other adjustments would be:

(i)   fixed assets should be revalued at market values and classified as current
(ii) stocks should be valued at liquidation values
(iii) any liquidated damages relating to unfulfilled sales or purchase contracts should be recognised
(iv) any redundancy or termination indemnities payable to personnel have to be recognised
(v) all deferred costs have to be written off.

Although this case relates specifically to a company which has never been a 'going concern', similar basic principles would apply in the case of a company which had been profitable but was now having cash flow difficulties.

E (2) - UNIVERSAL PLASTICS LIMITED: FRAUD INVESTIGATION

(a) The Cash Payments System

(a) How could Makepeace have made improper payments?

The only evidence the company had of who had actually been paid was the duplicate credit-transfer list sent to the bank; the original might easily have been different. The bank would pay on the evidence of the original, not of the duplicate. Particularly as far as the 'rush' payments were concerned, there was no-one other than Makepeace concerned in preparing them; he could well have typed one thing on the top copy going to the bank, and another on the duplicate retained for the company's records.

(b) Why would this system not have been discovered?

If Makepeace made the duplicate payments list out for a payment to a real supplier in respect of items already supplied and paid for, then who could find out that the payment had been made twice (especially if the invoice was rendered in duplicate—as many are)? And there would be plenty of evidence to show that it had been a payment made in respect of goods actually ordered, actually paid for and actually used in the business.

(c) What would you do to investigate this hypothesis?

(i) Call for several years' original payment lists from the bank (they would have them somewhere). Check them off against the company's duplicates. If the hypothesis is correct, some payees will be different (though the amounts will be the same). Look especially at the rush lists prepared by Makepeace himself.

(ii) Prepare statements at least for the principal suppliers showing the details (over quite a long period) of what we have paid for them, and what invoices we have paid. This will show that we have paid some invoices more than once (if the hypothesis is correct).

(iii) Prepare statements at the latest convenient date after Makepeace's departure for all suppliers showing the amount and details that, according to *our* books, are due to them. Send them direct to the suppliers and ask them to confirm their correctness or otherwise, direct to the auditors. (N.B. There may have been someone other than Makepeace involved at the company.)

E (2) - UNIVERSAL PLASTICS LIMITED: FRAUD INVESTIGATION

(b) How Makepeace Did It

(a) The audit checks that might have found it

(i) By far the best one would have been to have asked the bank for a selection of the original credit-transfer payments lists retained in their possession, and to have compared them with the duplicates in the company's possession. The bank may be 'reluctant' as stated here, to send these back regularly, but at the client's request (prompted by the auditors) they may well be prepared to dig out a sample for the purposes of the audit.

(ii) Arrange with the directors for a selection of current credit-transfer payments to be checked by the auditors *after* they have been signed and *before* they are either handed back to Makepeace or posted. This is of limited value, since if Makepeace knew the auditors were on the premises (which he certainly would) he might well not be tempted to perpetrate anything dishonest at that time; but it is better than nothing, and we are sometimes reduced to this in default of anything better.

(iii) Take a sample of paid invoices all for the one supplier and check them all in depth to orders and GRNs. If one had picked Amalgamated Plasticisers one might have been lucky enough to find the duplicated payments.

(iv) Taking the reconciliation of the purchases shown by the nominal ledger and the goods received into stores shown by the costing system, and not letting it go until one had found out exactly why it did not reconcile. It should! That's what it is for.

(b) Recommendations on improving the system

(i) Bank to be persuaded to return the original credit-transfer list duly stamped to someone in the company other than the person sending it off to the bank (i.e. *not* to Makepeace). This is the only outside evidence there is of who had actually been paid.

(ii) The signed credit-transfer list and letter to the bank to be dispatched direct to the bank by the signatories or their secretaries. Why should Makepeace get it back? He should have been finished with it at that point.

(iii) GRNs and orders both cross-referenced to invoices, as well as vice-versa. If this were done in the stores and buying departments instead of in accounts they would have seen that the duplicated payment had in fact already been paid. This is the only check there can be in a voucher-payment system to see that nothing is paid for twice. This check should be done by a person independent of Makepeace.

(iv) The system for rush payments should be not less fool-proof than the system for regular payments; the risk is no less.

(v) No-one but the machinists to operate the ledger machines; lock them at night.

(vi) There should be an invoice register, showing cross-references to orders, GRNs and payments. This would at least have made the duplicated payments more liable to detection; the secretary should have examined it periodically for this (and other) reasons.

(vii) Duplicates of purchase invoices rendered in a number of copies should be retained in the buying department or destroyed; what did the accounts department need them for?

(viii) The duties of paying creditors should be periodically rotated. This might not have prevented the fraud, but it would have added to the risk that Makepeace was running; his replacement could easily have looked back at the payments already made to Amalgamated Plasticisers, in order to avoid duplication.

(ix) There should have been an integrated costing system, tying up what was paid for in total with what was received.

(x) A reconciliation should be made of suppliers' statements with invoices and payments made, ensuring that all payments recorded in the cash book to any one supplier appear on a statement.

N.B. A Warning Wherever one man is in complete charge of payments, and there is no independent evidence of what person actually received the payment (e.g. a returned cheque), there is always room for fraud. This is increased on a voucher-payment system, where the possibilities of detecting duplicate payments are very much less.

E (2) - UNIVERSAL PLASTICS LIMITED: FRAUD INVESTIGATION

(c) The Understatement of Creditors

(i) *Check on cut-off!*
Goods received before the balance sheet date; were they included in creditors? Check entries in GRNs shortly before 31 March and see that they are either included in payments before, or creditors outstanding at, the year end.

(ii) In a voucher-payment system, it is not only relevant to see that an outstanding item was not paid till the new year; it is also necessary to see that it was *not* paid before.

(iii) Why were April invoices being paid in *April*? They weren't due to be paid till *May*. In looking through the payments after date (to pick up outstandings) one should also be looking to see that what was paid was due to be paid—and not (apparently) being paid early.

(iv) Looking through the previous April and May payments would have revealed an unusual number of debit and credit notes adjusting amounts paid to suppliers. Why? Did the company not know the right amount to pay?

(v) It should have been in the auditor's mind that if we had regular deliveries from a regular supplier, there ought to have been an outstanding item at the end of the year from him. Where was it?

(vi) Direct confirmation of amounts outstanding with the principal suppliers would have exposed the fraud. What reliance could be placed on the company's having checked suppliers' statements, when Makepeace asserted that they were too difficult to reconcile and threw them away?

(vii) Compare levels of creditors to the previous year and enquire into any unusual fluctuations and also calculate the ratio of trade creditors to cost of sales and enquire into fluctuations from previous periods.

(viii) The company should have had a proper system for identifying all invoices paid after, but referable to before, the year end. They should, say, have been stamped 'After date'; the buying department should have prepared a list of all GRNs received up to 31 March which had not been matched with invoices before then; the stock-taking instructions should have covered the point. Quite inadequate to rely *only* on Makepeace going through the invoices himself; the dates of invoices are often misleading, and he could not possibly know of his own knowledge what items had actually been received and taken into stock. The system should supply built-in checks on this.

E (2) - UNIVERSAL PLASTICS LIMITED: FRAUD INVESTIGATION

(d) Inflating the Stock Figure

(a) Audit steps with a chance of discovering the fraud

(i) Checking the opening balances on the new stock cards to the rough count sheets, and vice versa; are they starting the new year off right?

(ii) Scrutinising the rough stock sheets to see, *inter alia*, if any surprising number seen to be written up in the same hand. Was Makepeace one of the stock-taking team? Who purported to have taken stock with him?

(iii) Counting all stock of one type at the physical inventory attendance, to check through on the final stock sheets that that is the only quantity of that type there included—i.e. that there is nothing more.

(iv) Why were there so few queries on the lines that Makepeace had written up? There seemed to be plenty elsewhere.

(v) If there were no entries on the fraudulent stock cards near the year-end, did these stocks not look a bit slow-moving? (See Case E(2)(d), paragraph 4, in the companion volume to this book *Cases in Auditing Practice* (3rd edition)).

(vi) Importance of never confining any type of test to only one part of the year—e.g. testing ins and outs on the stock cards with the underlying documents (See Case E(2)(d), paragraph 4).

(vii) Try to estimate the approximate amount of stock in hand in terms of production, storage space, value for insurance, talking to the storemen and so on. (This was the way all Makepeace's frauds were discovered.)

(b) Recommendation to prevent recurrence

(i) All rough stock sheets to be written in ink, pre-numbered, and accounted for when complete! Auditors to see this is done when they attend.

(ii) All the stock ledger cards to be numbered and accounted for. Supposing someone had dropped a tray—or just lost some cards?

(iii) Both rough and final stock sheets to be examined and initialled by the man in charge who really knows the stock. Silly mistakes can be—and regularly are—made in summarising rough stock sheets for pricing.

(iv) Discrepancies between physical and book stocks to be investigated and explained by the company. This would have left the auditors more time to get on with the audit.

(v) An integrated costing system, to account in total money values for all production going into finished stock, all sales coming out—and the balance in hand.

(vi) The directors and the distribution manager should have gone over the finished stock sheets, in detail and together. As it was, the directors criticised what was brought into their books—and the distribution manager defended what was actually in the warehouse. No meeting of minds. Management cannot afford to disregard the figures that summarise the facts they know.

E (2) - UNIVERSAL PLASTICS LIMITED: FRAUD INVESTIGATION

(e) The Auditor's Position

No specific solution is provided for this section of the case which is a matter for the judgement of participants. The cases cited below may provide some relevant additional material.

Kingston Cotton Mill Company, 1896.

Westminster Road Construction and Engineering Company Ltd., 1932.

McKesson & Robbins (U.S.A.), 1942.

Candler v *Crane, Christmas and Co*, C.A., 1951.

Hedley Byrne and Co Ltd v *Heller and Partners Ltd.*, 1964.

Thomas Gerrard and Sons Ltd., 1967.

For details of these cases see:

T.A. Lee, *Company Auditing: Concepts and Practices*, Gee, 1982.
E. Woolf, *Auditing Today*, Prentice-Hall International, 1979.

E (3) – RED LION HOTEL (SEALAND) LIMITED: SMALL COMPANY AUDIT

(a) Accounting System for Purchasing and Payments

See pages 96-99.

RED LION HOTEL (SEALAND) LIMITED

PERIOD ENDED 30th SEPTEMBER, 1983   PURCHASING AND

Narrative	Op. No.	Requisioners
Requisitioner makes a note of order which has been approved by Mr Little (verbally). Mr Little places order by a telephone call to supplier.	1	
Checks delivery note against note of order. Any differences notified to supplier by telephone and noted on delivery note. Initials delivery note.	2	
	3	
Mr Little initials for approval to pay subject to detailed checking	4	
	5	
Mr Grudgings checks delivery notes against invoices	6	
	7	
Mr Grudgings sorts invoices and checks them against suppliers' statements	8	
	9	
Mr Grudgings writes up the Bought Day Bood and Brough Ledger, invoices marked with the page number in the Day Book.	10	
	11	

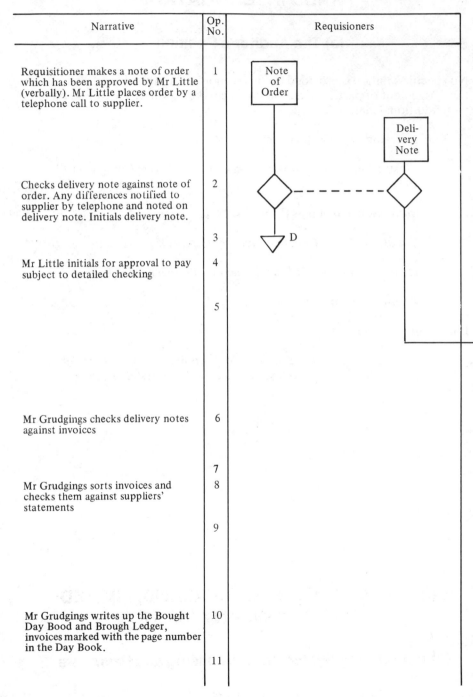

P1.1
Prepared by: S.D.S.
20.10.83

PAYMENTS

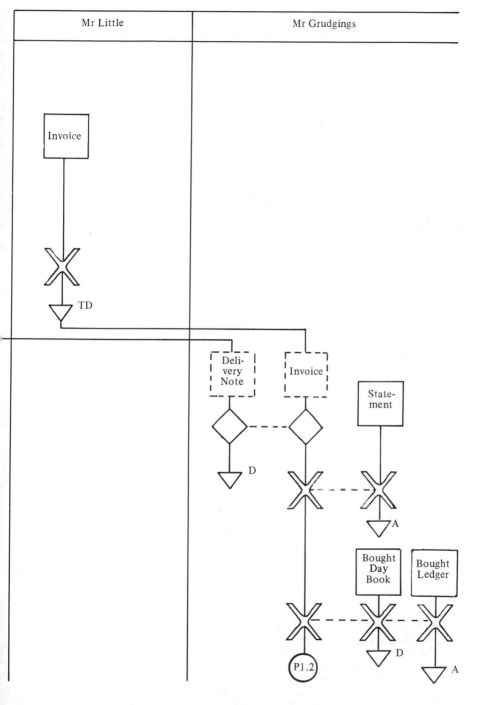

RED LION HOTEL (SEALAND) LIMITED

PERIOD ENDED 30th SEPTEMBER, 1983   PURCHASING AND

Narrative	Op. No.	Mr. Grudgings
		P1.1
		Invoice
Mr. Grudgings prepares cheque, marks invoice with the cheque number and passes both cheques and invoices to Mr Little	13	Cheque
Mr Little signs cheques after comparing odd invoices against cheques	14	
	15	
Mrs Little signs cheque (Note: If Mrs Little is away she signs a block of cheques)	16	A
Mr Grudgings enters cash book	17	Cash Book — To Supplier
Mr Grudgings prepares a bank reconciliation	18	Bank Statement — Bank Reconciliation
	19	D
	20	D
Mr Little reviews reconciliation and files	21	
	22	

P1.2
Prepared by S.D.S.
20.10.83

PAYMENTS

Mr. Little	Mrs. Little

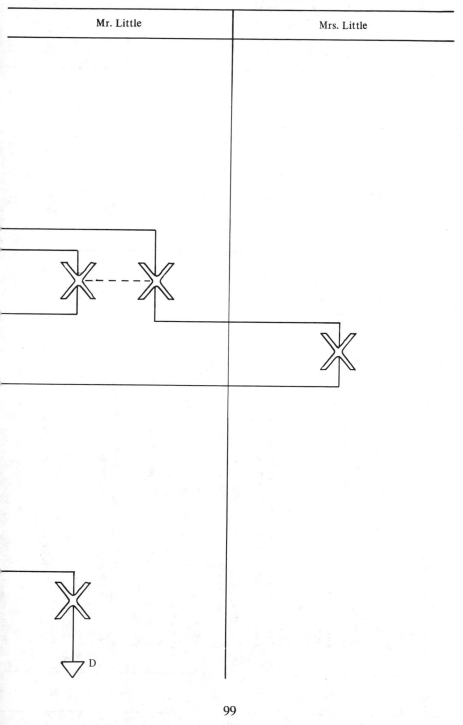

(b) Controls check list for small companies

POINT		19.83 Answer	19.83 Date / Initials	19. Answer	19. Date / Initials	19.. Answer	19.. Date / Initials
1	**MAIL**						
	(a) Is all mail received and opened by the proprietor?	Yes/No	[initials] 8|10|83	Yes/No		Yes/No	
	(b) If the proprietor does not himself open the mail, is it opened by a person not connected with the accounts (e.g. the proprietor's secretary) and read by him before it is distributed to the staff?	Not applicable Yes/No	8|10|83	Yes/No		Yes/No	
2	**RECEIPTS**						
	(a) Are all cheques and postal orders received by post counted by the proprietor before they are passed to the cashier?	Yes/No	[initials] 8|10|83	Yes/No		Yes/No	
	(b) Are all cheques and postal orders crossed to the company's branch of its bankers "Not negotiable – Accounts payee only"?	Yes/No	[initials] 8|10|83	Yes/No		Yes/No	
	(c) Are cash sales and credit sale receipts over the counter controlled by locked cash register tapes which only the proprietor can open?	Yes/No	[initials] 8|10|83	Yes/No		Yes/No	
	(d) Does the proprietor reconcile the cash register totals with the cash sales receipts daily?	Yes/No	[initials] 8|10|83	Yes/No		Yes/No	
	(e) Is the person performing the duties of cashier barred any responsibility concerning the sales, purchase or nominal ledgers?	Yes/No	[initials] 8|10|83	Yes/No		Yes/No	
3	**BANKING**						
	(a) Is all cash received banked intact at intervals of not more than three days? (except in winter = weekly)	Yes/No	[initials] 8|10|83	Yes/No		Yes/No	
	(b) Does the proprietor reconcile all monies received with the copy paying-in slips at regular intervals?	Yes/No	[initials] 8|10|83	Yes/No		Yes/No	

100

	PAYMENTS			
4	(a) Are all payments except sundry expenses made by cheque?	Yes/~~No~~ GS 8/10/83	Yes/No	Yes/No
	(b) Does the proprietor sign all cheques?	Yes/~~No~~ GS 8/10/83	Yes/No	Yes/No
	(c) Are cheques signed by the proprietor only after he has satisfied himself that:			
	i) he has approved and cancelled all vouchers supporting the payment?	~~Yes~~/No GS 8/10/83	Yes/No	Yes/No
	ii) all cheques are crossed:			
	– not negotiable?	~~Yes~~/No GS 8/10/83	Yes/No	Yes/No
	– account payee only?	~~Yes~~/No GS 8/10/83	Yes/No	Yes/No
	iii) all cheque numbers are accounted for?	~~Yes~~/No GS 8/10/83	Yes/No	Yes/No
	(d) Are petty cash expenses controlled by the imprest system?	~~Yes~~/No GS 8/10/83	Yes/No	Yes/No
	(e) Does the proprietor review all expenses and initial the petty cash book before reimbursing the cashier?	~~Yes~~/No GS 8/10/83	Yes/No	Yes/No
	BANK STATEMENTS			
5	(a) Are bank statements and paid cheques sent direct to the proprietor and opened only by him?	Yes/~~No~~ GS 8/10/83	Yes/No	Yes/No
	(b) Does the proprietor scrutinize all paid cheques to ensure that he has signed them all before he passes them to the cashier?	~~Yes~~/No GS 8/10/83	Yes/No	Yes/No
	(c) Does the proprietor:			
	i) prepare a bank reconciliation each month?	~~Yes~~/No GS 8/10/83	Yes/No	Yes/No
	or			
	ii) review in detail a reconciliation produced by the cashier?	~~Yes~~/No GS 8/10/83	Yes/No	Yes/No
	ORDERS			
6	(a) Are all purchase orders issued:			
	i) serially numbered by the printer?	~~Yes~~/No GS 8/10/83	Yes/No	Yes/No

		19 83			19..			19..	
		Answer	Date / Initials		Answer	Date / Initials		Answer	Date / Initials
7	**ORDERS** (Contd.)								
	ii) pre-printed duplicate order forms?	Yes/No	98 8/10/83		Yes/No			Yes/No	
	(b) Does the proprietor approve all orders?	Yes/No	98 8/10/83		Yes/No			Yes/No	
8	**RECEIPT OF GOODS** Are delivery notes:								
	(a) checked with goods?	Yes/No Not applicable	98 8/10/83		Yes/No			Yes/No	
	(b) compared with the copy order?	Yes/No	98 8/10/83		Yes/No			Yes/No	
	(c) compared with the invoice?	Yes/No	98 8/10/83		Yes/No			Yes/No	
9	**WAGES** (a) Is a separate cheque drawn for the exact amount to pay wages and national insurance?	Yes/No	98 8/10/83		Yes/No			Yes/No	
	(b) Does the proprietor either prepare or examine the wages records before signing the cheque?	Yes/No	98 8/10/83		Yes/No			Yes/No	
	(c) Does the proprietor initial the wages records after his examination?	Yes/No	98 8/10/83		Yes/No			Yes/No	
	DEBTORS (a) If credit is granted to customers, does the proprietor: i) authorise every extension of credit to a customer? or	Yes/No Yes/No	98 8/10/83 CC 8/10/83		Yes/No			Yes/No	

(b) Does the proprietor authorise all:				
i) write-offs of bad debts?	~~Yes/No~~ GS 8/10/83	Yes/No	Yes/No	
ii) sales returns and allowances?	~~Yes/No~~ GS 8/10/83	Yes/No	Yes/No	
iii) discounts other than routine cash discount? *Credit allowed only to tour operators*	~~Yes/No~~ GS 8/10/83	Yes/No	Yes/No	
(c) Does the proprietor receive a monthly list of debtors, showing the age of the debts?	~~Yes/No~~ GS 8/10/83	Yes/No	Yes/No	
(d) Are all authorisations by the proprietor evidenced by his initials?	~~Yes/No~~ GS 8/10/83	Yes/No	Yes/No	
GOODS OUTWARDS				
10 (a) Are pre-numbered despatch notes prepared for *all* goods leaving premises?	Yes/No N/A	Yes/No	Yes/No	
(b) Are all despatch notes:				
i) accounted for?	Yes/No GS	Yes/No	Yes/No	
ii) cross referenced with invoices and credit notes?	Yes/No 8/10/83	Yes/No	Yes/No	
(c) Is the proprietor satisfied that all goods leaving the premises have been accounted for?	Yes/No	Yes/No	Yes/No	
STOCK Does the proprietor scrutinize the stocks regularly to:				
(a) keep abreast of what is in stock?	Yes/~~No~~ GS 8/10/83	Yes/No	Yes/No	
(b) discover obsolete items?	Yes/~~No~~ GS 8/10/83	Yes/No	Yes/No	
(c) discover damaged articles?	Yes/~~No~~ GS 8/10/83	Yes/No	Yes/No	
(d) ensure that stock levels are kept under control?	Yes/~~No~~ GS 8/10/83	Yes/No	Yes/No	

COMPANY NAME . . . . Red Lion Hotel (Sealand) Limited . . . . . . File No. . . . .

(c) Vouching Audit Programme

Section 2 — Cash Book

The purpose of audit tests on cash is to establish that:

    (a) the cash book is a reliable record of the cash transactions;

    (b) for receipts —
        (i) all cash that should have been received has been received at the appropriate time, and
       (ii) all cash received has been applied to the client's benefit immediately;

    (c) for payments —
        (i) all expenditure is for the purpose of the client's business;
       (ii) payment is made only against documents which have been approved for payment by an appropriate official;
      (iii) payment is made only when sanctioned by the responsible person; and
      (iv) payment is made to the proper payee;

    (d) control procedures consistent with the client's organisation and size are applied over cash transactions.

Bank Reconciliation

Bank reconciliations should be made by either:

    (a) a person independent of the cashier, or

    (b) by the cashier but reviewed in detail by an independent official who initials the reconciliation as evidence of his review.

These are invaluable in ensuring the reliability of the cash records, since they confirm that the cash records are supported by independent records maintained by the firm's bankers. Regular reconciliations are, therefore, an essential feature of good procedures in relation to cash control. The reconciliations should be retained on a file for reference purposes.

POINT		19..		19..		19..	
		Sch. Ref.	Date Initials	Sch. Ref.	Date Initials	Sch. Ref.	Date Initials
201	Read Controls checklist, and any system notes and familiarise yourself with the system of accounting and control in operation over cash. Note especially any weaknesses.						
202	BANK RECONCILIATIONS Review the file of bank reconciliations and ensure that regular reconciliations have been made. If no reconciliation is made, note on a schedule and draw to the manager's attention.						
203	Select one reconciliation and check all items in reconciliation at the end of the period through to the following period. If any items are still not cleared, prepare a schedule detailing the items and obtain satisfactory explanations as to the nature of each item. File the schedule on the current audit file.						
204	In addition to the year-end work, compare cash book and bank statements in detail for the selected periods of . . . . . weeks/months, clearing both records for the periods chosen. At least one of the periods selected should cover a periodical reconciliation.						
205	Schedule any contra items appearing in the cash book or bank statements in the periods selected and obtain satisfactory explanations for each item. File the schedule on the current audit file.						
206	RECEIPTS Select . . . . .per cent of the receipts in each of . . . . .month(s) per quarter/half year and vouch as follows:- (a) Check entries with detailed cash receipts records if such are kept (e.g. daily cash summaries, till rolls, agents' cash sheets). If a rough cash book is kept by the official responsible for opening the post, the details shown therein should be traced into the cash book. Ensure that all items in the detailed records relating to the selected period have been recorded in the cash book.						

POINT		19.. Sch. Ref.	19.. Date Initials	19.. Sch. Ref.	19.. Date Initials	19.. Sch. Ref.	19.. Date Initials
206 cont'd	(b) When carbon copy or counterfoil receipt books are kept, check entries with copy or counterfoil receipts. Verify that the serial numbers run consecutively. Inquire into any missing numbers and inspect the cancelled originals and copies.						
	(c) Check postings to sales ledger.						
	(d) Trace receipts of cash from other bank and petty cash books.						
	(e) Where appropriate, check deductions from wages and salaries with wage sheets and salaries books. (No further work should be done on these items at this stage as they form the subject of vouching tests under other sections of the programme.)						
	(f) Vouch other receipts with correspondence or other documentary evidence and check postings to ledger accounts.						
	(g) Check the receipts shown in the cash book in detail with the copy paying-in slips stamped and initialled by the bank, observing that all receipts are banked intact daily. When checking the receipts with the paying-in slips, identify the amounts paid in with the individual items recorded in the cash book. Any alterations in the paying-in slips should receive special scrutiny.						
	(h) Obtain a small number of the *original* paying-in slips from the bank and compare the items in detail with the cash book.						
207	Check the additions of periods chosen for test.						
208	Check postings to the nominal ledger (including control accounts) for the months covering the periods selected.						
209	Trace to the nominal ledger the total cash discount for the months covering the periods selected for test and see that the total debit for discount bears a reasonable relationship to the cash received for the						

POINT		19..		19..		19..	
		Sch. Ref.	Date Initials	Sch. Ref.	Date Initials	Sch. Ref.	Date Initials
	month. Test that discounts allowed during the periods selected for test have been calculated in accordance with the company's terms.						
210	Scrutinise periods not covered by vouching tests and schedule items which appear to be of a special or unusual nature. Vouch these items and check the postings. File the schedule on the current audit file.						
211	Examine, on a surprise basis, the amount to be paid into the bank. Ensure that the following basic principles of internal control have been operated:- (a) Cheques received should have been crossed to the company's bankers at the time of opening the post. (b) Cash sales should have been reconciled with cash sales notes or till rolls. (c) All receipts (whether by post, from travellers or cash sales) should have been recorded in the cash book and be about to be paid into the bank intact. (d) If the above controls are not being operated, prepare a schedule of the position and bring to the attention of the manager. File the schedule on the current audit file.						
212	Complete the conclusion schedule.						
213	CHEQUE PAYMENTS Select. 10 per cent of the payments in each of ..3... month(s) *chosen at random per half year* and vouch as follows:- (a) With paid cheques crossed — 'account payee only — not negotiable'. (b) If payments are effected by means of traders' credits, vouch with cheques drawn in favour of the banks concerned, supported by the duplicates of the detailed lists of suppliers to be credited duly stamped by the bank. Bearer cheques must not be accepted						

POINT	19..		19..		19..	
	Sch. Ref.	Date Initials	Sch. Ref.	Date Initials	Sch. Ref.	Date Initials
as evidence in support of any payment. The further vouching tests to be applied to the selected payments will depend on the nature of the payments.						
214 Purchases of goods and services. (a) Vouch with statements, verifying that all discounts to which the client is entitled have been taken. Examine the supporting invoices, verifying that the invoices are signed or initialled by Mr Little and that they are for goods supplied or services rendered that are necessary for the client's business. (b) Trace 50 per cent of the invoices inspected in each of the foregoing periods into the purchase day book and see that they have been correctly analysed under the appropriate expenditure classifications. Note: Where the system adopted makes tracing the invoices selected into the purchase day book impracticable, the programme should be amended so that a test is carried out of the entries in the purchase journal and ledgers. (c) Select 50 per cent of the invoices inspected in each of the foregoing periods for detailed checking. The items selected for test should be representative of each type of transaction.						
215 Prepare a schedule stating details of the items selected showing the tests to be carried out. On completion of the work, file the schedule on the current audit file.						
216 In respect of the selected items:- (a) check with delivery notes to show that the goods have been received in good order and condition or the services rendered satisfactorily;						

POINT	19.. Sch. Ref.	19.. Date Initials	19.. Sch. Ref.	19.. Date Initials	19.. Sch. Ref.	19.. Date Initials
(b) check calculations and additions of invoices; and (c) agree prices charged with suppliers' price lists or other evidence, if not quoted on order.						
217 Vouch wages, salaries, PAYE, national insurance and petty cash, where totals only are shown in the cash book and details in subsidiary books, with wages sheets, salaries sheets or other detailed records. (No further work should be done on these items at this stage as they form the subject of separate vouching tests.) In cases where round amounts are drawn to meet wages requirements, trace that the balance is promptly repaid into bank or petty cash.						
218 Trace transfers to the petty cash book ~~in the periods selected~~ into the cash book.						
219 Vouch other payments in the periods selected with invoices or other documentary evidence and check postings to ledger accounts.						
220 Check additions of periods chosen for test and check balances forward at end of each month.						
221 Check postings to the nominal ledger (including control accounts) for the months covering the periods selected.						
222 Trace the total cash discount received for the months covering the periods selected for test to the nominal ledger.						
223 Scrutinise cash payments book and list items which appear to be of a special or unusual nature, the list to be filed on the current audit file. Vouch these items and check the postings.						

POINT		19..		19..		19..	
		Sch. Ref.	Date Initials	Sch. Ref.	Date Initials	Sch. Ref.	Date Initials
224	Do the procedures, as set out in the permanent audit file and as operated by the client, observe the following basic principles of internal control? (a) The receipt of goods should be recorded on goods inward notes, or in a goods inward book, which should be checked against invoices when they are received. Goods returned should be controlled in a similar manner.	*Yes/ No		Yes/ No		Yes/ No	
	(b) Invoices and credit notes should be signed or initialled as approved by a director or senior official before they are entered in the books.	*Yes/ No		Yes/ No		Yes/ No	
	(c) With the exception of cheques for wages, petty cash and similar funds, all cheques should be crossed 'Account payee only — not negotiable'. In no circumstances should cheques be signed in blank.	*Yes/ No		Yes/ No		Yes/ No	
	(d) Invoices and other supporting documents should be presented to the cheque signatory with the cheques. After payment the supporting documents should be cancelled to prevent their use in support of further payments.	*Yes/ No		Yes/ No		Yes/ No	
	*Delete whichever is not applicable.						
225	If the answers in respect of any of the above matters is unsatisfactory, prepare a schedule of the unsatisfactory procedures, file it on the current audit file, and bring to the attention of the manager. Update the I.C.Q. for unsatisfactory procedures identified by audit tests.						
226	Complete the conclusion schedule. PETTY CASH AND POSTAGE						
227	Vouch the petty cash book for 10 weeks chosen at random throughout the year. The nature of the evidence to be seen will vary with the type of payments made, for example:- (a) receipted accounts and supporting invoices should be seen for payments to suppliers.						

POINT	19 . .		19 . .		19 . .	
	Sch. Ref.	Date Initials	Sch. Ref.	Date Initials	Sch. Ref.	Date Initials
(b) reimbursement of expenses incurred by staff, and small items, should be vouched with petty cash vouchers, supported by external documentary evidence wherever practicable; and						
(c) amounts transferred to postage books should be traced to those books;						
(d) vouch wages with wages sheets. (No further work should be done at this stage as they form the subject of separate vouching tests later).						
228 Check additions of periods vouched. Check balances forward at the end of each month and, at the same time, see that the balance in hand is not in excess of requirements.						
229 Check postings to the nominal ledger (including control accounts) for the months covering the periods selected.						
230 Scrutinise the petty cash book for the periods not covered by the vouching tests and vouch items of a special or unusual nature.						
231 Check the additions of the postage book for . . . . . . days spread over the year.						
232 Trace balances forward at the periodical balancing (if balanced frequently, test) and verify that the balance carried forward is not excessive.						
233 Scrutinise the postage book for two months chosen at random and see that the entries relate prima facie to the company's business and that there are no large or exceptional outgoings.						
234 Do the procedures, as set out in the permanent audit file and as operated by the client, observe the following basic principles of internal control?						

POINT	19..		19..		19..	
	Sch. Ref.	Date Initials	Sch. Ref.	Date Initials	Sch. Ref.	Date Initials
(a) Petty cash should normally be for cash expenses only. Suppliers' accounts, wages and commissions should not be paid through the petty cash.	*Yes/ No		Yes/ No		Yes/ No	
(b) Petty cash should be kept on the imprest system.	*Yes/ No		Yes/ No		Yes/ No	
(c) The petty cash float should be fixed at a reasonable level having regard to the level of expenses.	*Yes/ No		Yes/ No		Yes/ No	
(d) The petty cash book should be produced to the cheque signatory at the time the float is reimbursed and initialled by him.	*Yes/ No		Yes/ No		Yes/ No	
(e) Petty cash and postage books should be periodically examined by a senior official and the balances verified.	*Yes/ No		Yes/ No		Yes/ No	
(f) Proper supervision should be exercised over the use of the franking machine.	*Yes/ No		Yes/ No		Yes/ No	
*Delete whichever is not applicable.						
235 If the answers in respect of any of the above matters is unsatisfactory, prepare a schedule of the unsatisfactory features, to be filed on the current audit file, and bring to the attention of the manager.						
236 Complete the conclusion schedule.						
CASH COUNT *Petty cash and other funds* (See also para. 244) Note: At no time during the count must the auditor be left alone with the cash, nor must he ever remove cash from the custody of the cashier before making the count.						
237 Make a surprise count of all cash, cheques and postage and trading stamps, including the cash of all companies or welfare funds audited by the company's auditors and any documents such as canteen tickets and luncheon vouchers which can readily be converted into cash. All cash must be produced at the same time.						

POINT	19..		19..		19..	
	Sch. Ref.	Date Initials	Sch. Ref.	Date Initials	Sch. Ref.	Date Initials
237 cont'd Note details with date and time of count on a working paper, to be signed by the member of the staff who counted the cash, and place on the current audit file. Where there is also cash belonging to companies audited by other auditors, arrangements should be made with the auditors of those companies for them to carry out simultaneously a surprise count of cash belonging to such companies and, if this is not possible, the matter should be brought to the attention of the partner on points on accounts.						
238 Agree the total amount of the cash and cheques produced with the books of the client which must be written up to date in ink. Confirm by reference to recent cheque counterfoils that all cheques drawn to replenish the cash funds have been entered in the cash records.						
239 Agree the stocks of postage and trading stamps, with the appropriate records, which should be written up to date in ink.						
240 Verify that all cheques included in the cash counted are drawn in favour of the company and crossed 'Account payee only – not negotiable'.						
241 List all cheques produced and investigate the nature of the transactions to which they relate. Subsequently trace that all such cheques are paid into the bank without delay and duly met.						
242 List unentered vouchers forming part of the reconciliation and subsequently trace into the books of the client.						
243 Bring to the immediate attention of a senior official any unusual cheques and all IOUs. Make a note of such items, to be placed on the current audit file, and bring to the attention of the manager.						

POINT	19..		19..		19..	
	Sch. Ref.	Date Initials	Sch. Ref.	Date Initials	Sch. Ref.	Date Initials
STOCK OF RECEIPT BOOKS 244 Call for the stock of unused receipt books and verify the stock with the balance shown on the register of receipt books.						
245 Test purchases during the year with the suppliers' invoices and, where appropriate, obtain confirmation of purchases from printers. The manager's approval and the client's permission must be given before this confirmation is obtained.						
246 Ascertain that all departments to which books have been issued during the year have been subject to audit tests during the course of the year.						
247 Complete the conclusion schedule.						

(d) Management Letter

The Directors,
Red Lion Hotel (Sealand) Limited,
Hampshire.

Dear Sirs,

1.   Our examination of the company's system of
accounting and internal control has revealed certain
matters which we consider we should draw to your attention.
We recognise that the size of the company's staff precludes
a sophisticated system of control and that control in the
company relies largely on close personal supervision -
exercised by the directors - and have borne this in mind in
making our assessments.

2.   We are also taking this opportunity to suggest
suitable remedies which we hope you will feel able to
implement. We would like to make clear that the matters
discussed in this letter are those which we have discovered
in the course of our examination for the purpose of our audit.
This examination would not necessarily reveal every weakness
in your accounting or administrative procedures.

Cash receipts

3.   There is no independent control of cash receipts
since:

    (a)   the receptionists are responsible for receipt
        of cash payments, entry of cash received in the
        daily tabular sheet and the daily receipts
        cash book;

    (b)   all cheques and postal orders received by post
        are passed to the receptionists for entry into
        the daily receipts cash book without previous
        listing or crossing; and

    (c)   the receptionists are also responsible for
        preparation of paying-in slips and bankings.

        In these circumstances it is possible for receipts
to be misappropriated or remain unbanked without detection.

cont/.....

4.   We suggest that Mr Little should:

(a)   note the total of all monies received by
             post before he passes the cheques and
             postal orders to the receptionists;

(b)   cross all cheques and postal orders
             received by post 'Not negotiable -
             a/c payee only';

(c)   check at weekly intervals that:

     (i)   his record of total monies
             received by post agrees with
             the entries in the daily
             receipts cash book,

     (ii)   cash entries on the daily
             tabular sheet agree with the
             entries in the daily cash
             book,

     (iii)   the copy cash receipts in both
             sets of receipt books are in
             sequence and agree with the
             daily receipts cash book, and

     (iv)   the copy paying-in slips agree
             with the daily receipts cash
             book;

(d)   scrutinise the daily tabular sheets for
             obvious errors; and

(e)   initial the daily tabular sheets and the daily
             receipts cash book when he has carried out
             this check.

Cheque payments

5.   Control over cheque payments is inadequate
    since:

(a)   invoices and other supporting documents are
             not properly cancelled when payment has been
             made. It is therefore possible for invoices
             to be paid twice;

(b)   supporting documents for cheque payments are
             not presented to Mrs. Little for her
             information when she countersigns cheques.
             We also noted that on occasions Mrs. Little
             has signed cheques in blank. In these
             circumstances it is not possible for her to
             act as an effective check on irregular pay-
             ments since she will not be aware of the
             nature of the payments;

116

(c) cheques prepared by Mr. Grudgings are not crossed 'Not negotiable - a/c payee only'. It is therefore possible for cheques to be wrongly negotiated to other payees.

6. We recommend that:

(a) all supporting documents should be examined by Mrs. Little before she countersigns cheques;

(b) Mrs. Little should not sign cheques in blank. Where it is necessary to make a cheque payment in her absence, the bank should be instructed to honour cheques up to a specified amount on one signature only;

(c) all cheques, apart from wages or petty cash cheques, should be crossed 'Not negotiable - a/c payee only' before signature;

(d) all supporting invoices should be cancelled with the date and the cheque number before the cheques are signed by the cheque signatories; and

(e) cheques should be returned to Mr. Little for despatch to creditors.

Bank reconciliation

7. There is no independent review of the monthly bank reconciliation which is prepared by Mr. Grudgings, who is also responsible for preparation of cheques and cheque payments records. It is, therefore, possible for errors or misappropriations to remain undetected.

8. We recommend that Mr. Little should:

(a) examine all returned cheques before they are passed to Mr. Grudgings to ensure that they:

   (i) are properly signed by both cheque signatories, and

   (ii) have not been amended since signature;

and

cont/.....

117

    (b)   scrutinise the bank reconciliation and initial it when he has satisfied himself that all items in reconciliation are:

        (i)   entered in the cash book, and

      (ii)   cleared in the following bank statement.

Petty cash

9.   Weekly wages are at present paid out of the petty cash funds. The average amount held in the petty cash box is therefore much larger than is required for normal purposes. The risk of loss from casual theft or misappropriation of petty cash is higher than necessary. The risk is intensified as there is no systematic review of petty cash payments. Mr. Little reviews the petty cash book periodically but, since the review is not in great depth, it is possible for unauthorised payments to be made.

10.   We recommend that:

    (a)   petty cash should be controlled by the use of a small imprest and that all expenses be reviewed by Mr. Little when the float is reimbursed;

    (b)   wages should not be paid out of the imprest but should be drawn on a separate wages cheque;

    (c)   Mr Little should examine the wages book before the wages cheque is signed; and

    (d)   Mr. Little should initial the wages book when he is satisfied that the amounts are correct.

11.   We appreciate that our suggestions will involve Mr. Little in a certain amount of administrative time but are convinced that his time will be well spent in ensuring the smooth running of your administration and minimising the risk of loss by reducing the temptation placed in the way of your staff.

12.   If there are any points about which you are unclear, or any further matters which you would like to discuss, please let us know.

13.   For our records, would you please let us know what action you propose to take in relation to each of the suggestions set out in this letter.

14.   We would like to take the opportunity of thanking you and your staff for your co-operation during the course of our audit.

                      Yours faithfully

E (4) - BRAKSON MANUFACTURING LIMITED: REVIEW CASE INCLUDING MANAGEMENT LETTER

1. Memorandum on Internal Control

During the course of the audit of the company's accounts for the year to 31st January, 1982, certain weaknesses were noted in the company's internal control system. The weaknesses noted are set out below, together with suggestions for improvement.

The most important single contribution to good internal control arises from the division of duties between employees so that they act as a check upon each other. But recommendations below have been made within the practical limitations imposed by the small number of staff among whom duties can be shared.

(i) *Purchases and trade creditors*

The ability to issue official orders should be guarded more closely. It is suggested that pre-numbered pads of order forms be issued to each of the Directors and to Mr. Lawrence; they should keep these in safe custody and all order form numbers should be subsequently accounted for. If an additional copy of the order were produced and sent to the Ledger Clerk, the latter could accept suppliers' invoices for payment without reference back to the buyer except where there are queries.

A further copy of the purchase order should be sent to the receiving point as authority to accept goods on delivery. As rewriting is an opportunity for error, it is further suggested tentatively that this copy be used as a goods inwards note also; the receipt of the goods would be noted on it and it would then accompany the goods to the stores and then be sent to the Ledger Clerk. [If a large proportion of orders are met by instalment deliveries, the above suggestion will not be appropriate.] Any goods inwards notes that are created at the receiving point should be pre-numbered, and the number sequence should be independently accounted for.

The purchase day book does not fulfil any function which is not equally well satisfied by the file of invoices. The related orders and goods inwards notes should be attached to the invoices when they are sent to the Directors for cheque signing. Supporting documents should accompany cheques to the second signatory. At present the latter is merely attesting the signature of the first Director. Alternatively, if two scrutinies of the documents are not desired, one signature only should be required on cheques.

(ii) *Sales and trade debtors*

There is some lack of clarity in the system of charging for non-standard goods. It is suggested that all orders of this nature should be sent to Mr. Neal for approval of the modification charge or waiver of this.

119

There is some danger that orders may be fulfilled twice when a customer confirms in writing an order given to a salesman. It is suggested that salesmen ask customers to sign the salesman's order form instead as evidence of placing an order.

Credit status should be checked before availability of goods. The present credit check omits to scrutinise new customers, who will not feature on the list of bad payers known to the company. A positive credit check should be introduced, so that only orders from known sound customers are accepted without further investigation.

Opportunity for error occurs in the copying of order details on to a daily summary, then on to a delivery note, then to an invoice. It is suggested that the invoice be prepared from the orders or summary, and that two extra copies be made to act as a delivery note.

Goods returned notes should be pre-numbered and the sequence accounted for. At present credit notes are issued automatically for goods returned. This is not always appropriate, since repair and return to customer can often be carried out quickly. For this reason and because credit notes are a simple means of concealing defalcations, the issue of credit notes should be under the personal control of one of the Directors.

The sales day book gives no information that is not already available from the file of sales invoices. For convenience as well as control considerations, a sales ledger control account should be kept; if possible this should be kept by Mr. Neal on the basis of information supplied by the invoice typist and the person who opens the mail. It is inevitable that much of the financial business of the company will be in the hands of Mr. Lawrence; but it is unfair to him, however much of a trusted servant he is, to make it too easy for him to misappropriate the company's funds.

The irregularity of follow-up of slow-paying customers increases the danger of failing to collect debts due to the company. It is suggested that Mr. Lawrence should be given a time-table of action, including set procedures for keeping Mr. Neal informed and for restricting acceptance of further orders in certain circumstances.

(iii) *Cash receipts and payments*

Mail opening is an important duty as it is the only point at which effective control over cash receipts is possible. It is suggested that, in view of his other duties, Mr. Lawrence should not undertake this duty except in emergency; it should be carried out by one of the directors accompanied by a secretary who should list the cash and cheques as soon as mail is opened.

Cash on the premises is a security risk. Consideration should be given to paying it into the bank every day.

It is incompatible with his other duties in relation to cash for Mr. Lawrence to be a cheque signatory. The position would be eased if, as suggested above, only one signature was required on a cheque. After signing, cheques should be immediately dispatched by the signatory instead of being returned to Mr. Lawrence. This procedure would reduce the opportunity for unauthorised amendments to cheques. As bank reconciliation statements are in part a check on Mr. Lawrence, they should be prepared or at least checked regularly by Mr. Neal.

The 'PAID' stamp is impressed on invoices to prevent them from being used, inadvertently or by design, to support a duplicate payment. At present the cheque signatories have no assurance that every invoice is stamped when the related cheque is issued, and can only have this assurance if they apply the stamp themselves at the time of signing the cheque.

(iv) *Stock and work in progress*

A very high proportion of the value of the company's stock consists of timber stocks. This is stored in an open yard to which access is not restricted. It is suggested that site layout should be adjusted so that only the stores staff have access to it, and the storeman can then be held responsible for the safe custody of the stocks held there. Production is authorised by the Production Director on a works order which specifies the materials to be used. At present there is no system for checking the foreman's actual requisitions against the authorised works order. It is recommended that such a check should be introduced.

Time sheets prepared by each production worker are accepted as the basis for allocating labour cost to production batches, but they are not checked or approved. It is recommended that time sheets should be approved by the foreman, and occasionally reviewed by the Production Director.

2. Audit Programme (Extract)

(i) *Purchases and trade creditors*

(a) Ascertain current system in company. Amend auditor's records of system to bring these up-to-date. Evaluate effectiveness of system, and base the extent of audit tests on this evaluation.

(b) Test a sample of orders right through the system, starting from the purchase order and following through to the cash payment. Record in the working papers any instances where the system in force has not been followed.

(c) Obtain client's listing of unpaid invoices making up the total creditors on the balance sheet; test the list of invoices, noting that these are for goods received before the year-end and were not paid until after the balance sheet date.

(d) Test the balances with suppliers' statements, including all major suppliers and some to whom the client shows no outstanding liability at the year-end. Enquire into differences and note where these are not merely minor differences of timing.

(e) Examine goods inwards notes just before and just after year-end. Ascertain whether related liability has been recorded in the correct financial year.

(f) Test a sample of returns notes, noting whether credit notes have been recorded in respect of each.

(g) Record opinion on this section of the audit.

(ii) *Sales and trade debtors*

(a) Ascertain current system in company. Amend auditor's records of system to bring these up-to-date. Evaluate effectiveness of system, and base extent of audit tests on this evaluation.

(b) Test a sample of sales right through the system, starting with the orders and following through to the receipt of cash. Record in the working papers any instances where the system in force has not been followed.

(c) Test a sample of returns through the system from goods returned note to credit note to sales ledger and to the ultimate solution of the dissatisfaction with the goods.

(d) Test completeness of numerical sequences of invoices and credit notes.

(e) Obtain client's listing of balances making up the total debtors on the balance sheet; test the list to the sales ledger.

(f) Review for defalcations being covered by teeming and lading by:
testing transfers between debtors' accounts to ascertain reasons for transfer.
testing payments on account to individual items on paying-in slips.
testing sales ledger cash postings just after year-end to individual items on paying-in slips.

(g) Review for inflation of sales at year-end by:
examining invoices for last month and ascertaining whether large or unusual items are genuine sales.
testing invoices near end of year to despatch records to check that goods were despatched before year-end.
examining credit notes for period since balance sheet date and enquiring into large items, noting any reversals of sales in the previous year.

(h) Send audit statements to a sample of customers, requesting confirmation to the auditors of the balance due. Follow up and resolve all disputes and non-replies.

(i) Obtain clients' listing of overdue debts. Test this to ledger balances—looking especially for overdue debts in ledger *not* included in the listing. Discuss overdue accounts with client and then review adequacy of bad debt provision.

(j) Record opinion on this section of the audit.

(iii) *Cash receipts and payments*

(a) Ascertain current systems in company. Amend auditors' records of systems to bring these up-to-date. Evaluate effectiveness of system and base extent of audit tests on this evaluation.

(b) Test a sample of cash receipts, chosen if possible from lists prepared at the time mail is opened. Inspect remittance advices or covering letters. Trace to individual entries on paying-in slips stamped by bank. Check recording in cash book of these items. Check postings to sales ledger.

(c) Scan receipts for rest of year and investigate items of an unusual nature; record these items and their explanation in working papers.

(d) Test a sample of cash payments by cheque or credit transfer. Select from cash book and trace to paid cheques (or stamped credit transfer lists) and to invoices and other supporting documents. Note that supporting documents have been stamped 'PAID'. This last check will only be of relevance if the recommendation to have the paid stamp applied by cheque signatures at the time of signing is applied.

(e) Test completeness of numerical sequence of cheques used.

(f) Scan cheque payments for rest of year and investigate items of an unusual nature; record these items and their explanation in working papers.

(g) Obtain a certificate from the bank stating the balance at the balance sheet date. Agree this to client's bank reconciliation statement for this date.

N.B. *The reply from United Bank Limited is unsatisfactory in that it does not provide answers to all the questions included in the specimen confirmation request included in Institute Statement U 22.*

(h) Obtain a copy of client's year-end bank reconciliation for inclusion in audit working papers. Check all items on this—to cash book for balance per books, to subsequent bank statements for deposits not recorded and cheques not cleared. Investigate cheques not cleared at time of audit.

(i) Trace items on bank statements for a week before and a week after balance sheet date to cash book and cash book items to bank statements; note that all items which are unmatched at year-end appear on the bank reconciliation.

(j) Unless internal control is very strong now in this area, carry out bank reconciliation work as at (g), (h) and (i) for an interim date also.

(k) Record opinion on this section of the audit.

(iv) *Stock and work in progress*

(a) Obtain a copy of client's stocktaking instructions and ascertain, if not included in these instructions, how physical count quantities are processed to calculate stock amounts for the balance sheet.

(b) Attend client's physical stocktaking. Make clear to client that auditor is there to observe and not to take over the work or responsibility of the stocktaking. Note in audit working papers any weaknesses in stock count procedures and state there whether overall the count was properly carried out so as to give the expectation of reliable results.

(c) Make and record test counts at physical stocktaking. At the time ensure agreement with client's count, and later trace test counts on to client's stock sheets.

(d) Check that goods movements near to year-end have been recorded in the same financial period that physical move occurred, check purchase invoices to goods inwards notes before and after year-end; check goods inwards notes to purchase invoices before and after year-end. (Do not duplicate work if these steps have been carried out in connection with audit of creditors); check despatch records to sales invoices before and after year-end; check sales invoices to despatch records before and after year-end. (Do not duplicate work if some of this work has already been carried out in connection with audit of sales and debtors).

123

   (e) Test cost figures on client's stock sheets to suppliers' invoices or costing records. Test cost figures on stock sheets with those of previous year, concentrating on items of major value; investigate large differences.

   (f) Test batch costing records which have formed basis for pricing year-end stocks to approved invoices and employees' time sheets. Review basis of applying overheads to stocks to ascertain whether it is acceptable and consistent with the previous year; check application of this basis to the work in progress at year-end.

   (g) Review and test larger items of materials stock and work in progress to ascertain whether market value of any items is below cost.

   (h) Review treatment of obsolete and slow-moving stocks. Ascertain whether the client is operating an adequate system for the identification and valuation of these items. Test the list of such items prepared by client at year-end. Enquire also into items which were in this category in the previous year, and items noted at the time of observation of the physical inventory count, if these do not feature on the current list. Record opinion whether the amount written off obsolete and slow-moving stocks is adequate and reasonable.

   (i) Obtain a stock certificate signed by the relevant executive director.

   (j) Record overall opinion on this section of the audit.

     Note: *Clerical accuracy checks would also be needed on records in each of the four areas noted above; it has been assumed that all such checks would be prescribed in a single section of the audit programme not reproduced above.*

3. Audit File

(i) There is wide variation among auditors in the extent of the documentation of audit work and so in the volume of their working paper files. But working papers must be able to give evidence to outside challengers, and in larger firms, to partners and managers, that an adequate audit has been carried out. The present file fails this test on two counts:

   (a) There are no schedules relating to certain captions on the balance sheet, and these should be added to the file:

       Directors' loan accounts
       Share Capital
       Depreciation of plant and machinery
       Bad debt provision
       Cash in hand

     (If the schedules had been cross-referenced, the lack of support for some balance sheet items would have been made clear.)

   (b) The file gives no indication of the audit work performed in relation to the figures set out on the schedules. As it stands the file is no more than an analysis of the accounts. It is not possible to state in advance where additional schedules will be required to record the audit work and where this can be shown on the existing schedules, except that additional schedules will be needed for the audit of stock.

(ii) See the following schedules.

(iii) A stock certificate is a formal statement by the director that he and his fellow-directors have discharged their responsibilities in relation to stock. These responsibilities have been summarised as follows (Institute Statement on Auditing U2, paragraph 4):

    (a) to ensure that the physical quantities owned by the company are properly ascertained and recorded.

    (b) to ensure that the condition is properly judged.

    (c) to ensure that the amount to be carried forward in the balance sheet has been properly determined on an appropriate basis or appropriate bases by suitable methods.

The stock certificate obtained from Mr. Neal should cover the substance of these three responsibilities. It should be noted that 'as valued by the Managing Director' is not of itself a satisfactory basis of determining the amount of stock; the basis used by the Managing Director needs to be specified.

(iv) A stock certificate does not constitute the end of an auditor's duties in relation to stock but rather its beginning. It is a formal, explicit statement of representations in respect of stock which are implied in the accounts themselves. It is the duty of the auditor to arrive at an independent professional opinion on the directors' representations about stock as well as about other items in the accounts. It is the complexity of determining and of checking the amount of stock which makes the obtaining of a certificate a helpful additional practice for this particular item.

BRAKSON MANUFACTURING LTD
FIXED ASSETS SUMMARY — VII

ACCOUNTS TO 31st JANUARY 1982

			BALANCE 31 JAN 81	ADDITIONS CURRENT DEPRECIATION	SALES	BALANCE 31 JAN 82	
			£	£	£	£	
COST							
PLANT AND MACHINERY			50,679	217 Sch VIII	–	50,896	
FIXTURES AND FITTINGS			1,972	278 Sch VIII	–	2,250	
VANS AND CARS		Sch IX	6,400	1,200	1,000	6,600	
	TOTAL		59,051	1,695	1,000	59,746	
AGGREGATE DEPRECIATION							
PLANT AND MACHINERY			20,760	6,362 Sch III	–	27,122	
FIXTURES AND FITTINGS			910	225 Sch IV	–	1,135	
VANS AND CARS		Sch IX	2,800	1,650	750	3,700	
	TOTAL		24,470	8,237	750	31,957	
TOTAL NET BOOK AMOUNT			34,581 + 1695 – 8237 –		250 =	27,789	
			Sch II			Sch II	

WORK DONE :

1) Balances at 31st January 1981 agreed to 1981 audit working papers.

2) Balances at 31st January 1982 agreed to general ledger and to plant Register totals.

3) Items selected from plant register identified with items physically verified on the company's premises.

4) Depreciation basis and calculations reviewed; bases are unchanged from 1981 and are reasonable in relation to expected lives and pattern of usage of assets.

BRAKSON MANUFACTURING LTD.,
ADDITIONS TO FIXED ASSETS

VIII

ACCOUNTS TO 31ST JANUARY 1982

£

PLANT AND MACHINERY

27 MAY 1981   CROSS CUT SAW   √φf π   217·32

Sch VII

FIXTURES AND FITTINGS

23 JUNE 1981	ELECTRIC TYPEWRITER	√φf π	208·57
20 AUGUST 1981	FILING CABINET	√φf	45·68
17 SEPTEMBER 1981	TYPIST'S CHAIR	√φf	24·19
			278·44

Sch VII

√   Evidence of Authorization to purchase seen
φ   Purchase invoice inspected
f   Traced to entry in Plant Register
π   Physically inspected

BRAKSON MANUFACTURING Ltd
VANS AND CARS

IX

ACCOUNTS TO 31st JANUARY 1982

	COST				AGGREGATE		DEPRECIATION	
	BALANCE 31 JAN 81	ADDITIONS	SALES	BALANCE 31 JAN 82	BALANCE 31 JAN 81	CURRENT EXPENSE	SALES	BALANCE 31 JAN 82
	£	£	£	£	£	£	£	£
CARS								
AXV 407	1,600			1600^{π}	800	400		1200
BMF 103	1,400			1400^{π}	350	350		700
						750 SCH IV		
VANS								
GKD 137	1000		1000^{δ}	..	750	–	750	–
DPG 812	1210			1210^{π}	600	300		900
LBJ 621	1190			1190^{π}	300	300		600
ADH 34	–	$1200 \sqrt{\phi}F$		1200^{π}	–	300		300
SCH VII	6400	1200	1000	6600	2800		750	3700
							＊	

aggregate depreciation on
       van sold   750   ＊
net book amount   250
proceeds of sale   200   φ
loss on sale   50 ——————→ 50
     Depreciation and loss on sale of vans   950   SCH IV

√   Evidence of authorization to purchase seen.
φ   Purchase invoice inspected — Trade in value of van sold verified
F   Traced to entry in Plant Register.   from it.
δ   Evidence of authorization of sale seen.
π   Vehicle Registration Sheets inspected; all registered
     in the name of the company.